RN BATTLESHIPS &
BATTLECRUISERS
IN FOCUS

Cdr David Hobbs MBE RN (Retd)

First published in the United Kingdom in 2009 by Maritime Books, Lodge Hill, Liskeard, Cornwall, PL14 4EL

INTRODUCTION

For centuries the line-of-battle ship was the final arbiter of sea power, a ship so powerful that only another like it could hope to fight it with any hope of success. The century of iron and steel ships between WARRIOR and VANGUARD saw some odd prototypes as nineteenth century technology advanced and also some powerful ships of majestic appearance. It also saw the type's gradual eclipse as aircraft carriers, submarines, mines and missiles assumed greater importance.

This book in the 'RN Ships in Focus' series contains photographs of many of the 188 battleships and battle-cruisers built by Britain between 1860 and 1960. The Table at the end of this book gives individual ship names and details such as full load displacement, length, horse-power, speed, main armament and cost to show how these ships developed. The photograph captions give a brief idea of individual histories and features.

All the ships were designed and built in Imperial measurement and I have used this throughout with abbreviations to save space. These include hp for horse-power; lb for pounds and pdr for 'pounder' in terms of shell weight. When referring to guns, MLR is short for Muzzle-Loading Rifled and BL for Breech-Loading. The term calibre denotes the internal diameter of a gun barrel measured in inches but, when describing the bigger guns, I have also used it in its other sense to express the length of the barrel. The length of the barrel is divided by the internal diameter to give a value, for instance 12" 40 calibre or 15" 42 calibre; the former being 40' long, the latter 52.5'.

David Hobbs
Twyford
2009

HMS WARRIOR was the first battleship to have a hull built of iron and was originally rated as a frigate because her forty guns were mounted on a single deck. She was built at Mare's Yard at Blackwall on the Thames and was launched by Sir John Pakington on 29 December 1860; it was a cold day and it took six tugs an hour to haul her off the frozen slipway. Her ten boilers worked at only 20psi. During her twenty year operational career, she escorted the Royal Yacht that carried Princess Alexandra from Denmark to marry the Prince of Wales in 1864 and towed a floating dock from Madeira to Bermuda in 1869. After years as a training hulk and use as a pier for an oil pipeline at Pembroke Dock, she survived into the modern era and has been fully restored. She is now open to the public in Portsmouth Historic Dockyard and has a claim to be both the first and the last British battleship of her era.

(T. Ferrers-Walker Collection)

HMS AGINCOURT was one of two '50-gun frigates' intended to carry the heaviest armament afloat behind the thickest armour at the highest sea speed. She was built by Laird's Yard in Birkenhead and completed on 1 June 1867. Armament included four 9-inch MLR and twenty-four 7-inch MLR and her armour, up to 5-inches thick, covered the whole hull above the waterline. In her active career between 1868 and 1889 she flew the flags of 15 different admirals and was nearly lost when she ran aground off Gibraltar in 1871. She formed part of the boys' training establishment HMS GANGES between 1905 and 1909 and then became a coal hulk at Sheerness. She too had a remarkably well-found hull and survived into the 1950s as the coal hulk C109 before being scrapped.

(T. Ferrers-Walker Collection)

HMS SCORPION was built by Laird's Yard in Birkenhead and completed on 10 October 1865 armed with four 9-inch MLR guns, the heaviest weapons then in service with the Royal Navy. The guns were laid and trained by hydraulic power but it took nearly an hour to move from maximum depression to maximum elevation. Her bunkers contained 336 tons of coal giving an endurance of 1,210 miles at 10 knots. After serving in the Channel Fleet for four years, she became the Bermuda guardship from 1870 and spent 30 years in the role. This 1897 photograph shows her in Bermuda with the original sailing rig removed and replaced by pole masts. She was sunk as a gunnery target in 1901, raised in 1902 and sold for scrap in 1903. Unfortunately, she foundered under tow to the breaker's yard in Boston, USA and sank for the second time, this time permanently.

(T. Ferrers-Walker Collection)

HMS LORD WARDEN was one of a group of lighter battleships intended to lower construction costs. They had wooden hulls covered by iron plates and were the heaviest and fastest wooden ships ever built. She was completed at Chatham in 1867 and was flagship of the Mediterranean Fleet from 1869 to 1875, seeing action against Spanish pirates. She was modernised in 1884 but a year later her hull was found to be rotten and her ship's company transferred to HMS DEVASTATION. She was condemned in 1889 and subsequently broken up, an early indication that cost-cutting measures can actually prove to be expensive when applied.

(T. Ferrers-Walker Collection)

HMS HERCULES was built in Chatham Dockyard and armed with eight 10-inch MLR guns in a central, armoured battery. The end guns could be traversed to fire nearly along the ship's centreline through the cutaway ports visible in the ship's side. Each gun weighed 18 tons and could fire a 400lb shell at a rate of one round about every 70 seconds. She served first with the Channel Fleet and towed HMS AGINCOURT off the Pearl Rock near Gibraltar in 1871 and was Flagship of the Mediterranean Fleet between 1875 and 1877. Modernisation between 1892 and 1893 included the removal of the sailing rig. The photograph shows her in the Reserve Fleet at Portsmouth after 1893 with glazed windows in the gun-ports.

(T. Ferrers-Walker Collection)

HMS REPULSE was the last British battleship to have a hull made basically of wood, albeit covered with iron plates. She was armed with twelve 8-inch MLR guns plus four torpedoes. Completed in 1870, she served first as guardship at Queens-ferry and then flagship of the Pacific Squadron based on the west coast of America, policing an area from British Columbia in the north to Patagonia in the south. She returned to the UK in 1877 under sail rather than steam, becoming the only British armoured battleship ever to round Cape Horne under canvas. After a period in reserve she was sold for scrap in 1889.
(T. Ferrers-Walker Collection)

HMS IRON DUKE was built in Pembroke Dockyard and completed in 1871. She gained a reputation for being one of the steadiest gun platforms in the fleet, became flagship of the China Station from 1871 and was the first capital ship to use the Suez Canal. She returned to the UK in 1875, when she accidentally rammed and sank the battleship VANGUARD. After modernisation she returned to the China Station as flagship between 1878 and 1883. She is seen here in dry-dock in Nagasaki carrying out a period of self-maintenance. After a period in reserve she was used as a coal-hulk at the Kyles of Bute after 1900 and broken up in 1906.

(T. Ferrers-Walker Collection)

HMS AUDACIOUS served as flagship of the China Station from 1875 to 1878 and again from 1883 to 1889. She is seen here in 1886 with her hull painted in the China Station's white paint scheme. After service as a guardship at Hull and in reserve she was renamed HMS FISGARD from 1902 to 1914. On the outbreak of war she was towed to Scapa Flow where she was again renamed as the depot ship HMS IMPERIEUSE until 1918 when she was towed to Rosyth to perform similar duties. She was sold for scrap in 1929.

(T. Ferrers-Walker Collection)

HMS SULTAN under both sail and steam in 1886. The complication of doing so, with the inherent risk of sparks from the two funnels setting fire to the sails is obvious. She was built in Chatham Dockyard and completed in 1871 with eight 10-inch MLR guns mounted on the broadside and four 9-inch guns a deck higher. Her weight of broadside was 2,240lb. In 1889 she ran aground and sank in the Comino Channel (Malta) but was subsequently raised and repaired. Her sailing rig was removed during a modernisation in 1893 when quick-firing light guns were added. After that she was maintained in the Portsmouth reserve fleet until 1906 when she was hulked as part of HMS FISGARD IV until 1931 when she became a mechanical repair ship. Between 1940 and 1945 she was used as a depot ship for minesweepers in Portsmouth. She was finally broken up in 1947. *(T. Ferrers-Walker Collection)*

HMS GLATTON was one of the first capital ships to be built with no sailing rig and a main armament concentrated in a revolving turret. She was known at first as a 'breastwork monitor' and was intended for coastal operations. The turret contained two 12-inch MLR guns, each of which weighed 25 tons and armour plate made up one third of her hull weight, a greater percentage than any previous British warship. She also had the lowest freeboard, making her a 'wet' ship in almost any sea-state. Built in Chatham Dockyard, she was completed in 1872 and spent most of her life in the reserve fleet in Portsmouth. She was reduced to extended reserve in 1901 and broken up in 1903.   *(T. Ferrers-Walker Collection)*

HMS DEVASTATION was the first iron ship to be built at Portsmouth Dockyard. She was completed in 1873 with turrets, heavy armour and no sailing rig. The armour on the turret and the ship's side was up to 12-inches thick and each of her four 12-inch MLR guns used a 110lb charge to fire a 706lb shell. The turrets were steam-trained and the guns hand-worked requiring a crew of 22 men in each. She served in the Mediterranean Fleet from 1874 to 1878 after which she went into reserve until 1885 when she became guard ship at Queensferry. In 1893 she became guardship at Devonport until 1898, then guardship at Gibraltar. She was reduced to reserve in Portsmouth in 1902 and sold for scrap in 1908.

(T. Ferrers-Walker Collection)

HMS GORGON was built by Palmers on the Tyne and completed in 1874 as a 'coast-defence' ironclad intended for the local defence of ports and anchorages. She was used as a tender to HMS CAMBRIDGE, the gunnery school at Devonport after completion but commissioned fully at Portland during the 'war scare' of 1878. She returned to training duties later in 1878 and was used in the annual manoeuvres until 1892. Widely thought to be a flawed design incapable of operation in the open sea, she was sold for scrap in 1903. *(Syd Goodman Collection)*

HMS DREADNOUGHT took seven years to build in Pembroke Dockyard and was completed in 1879; the first British warship to have artificial ventilation, longitudinal bulkheads and compound steam engines but the last to have armour plate over the entire hull area above the waterline. 1,800 tons of coal in her bunkers gave her a potential endurance of 5,700 miles at 10 knots. Each of her 12.5-inch guns weighed 38 tons. She went into the Reserve Fleet on completion and then joined the Mediterranean Fleet in 1884. In 1894 she became the Coastguard ship at Bantry until 1897 when she was re-fitted and re-engined at Chatham. She formed part of HMS DEFIANCE at Devonport in 1902 and was broken up for scrap in 1908.

(T. Ferrers-Walker Collection)

HMS INFLEXIBLE was a 'one-off' design built in Portsmouth Dockyard and completed in 1881 with two turrets, each of which contained two 16-inch MLR guns, the heaviest guns afloat at the time. Her armour was 24-inches thick, the thickest ever fitted in a Royal Navy warship before or since. She was the first battleship to have an armoured deck below the waterline in place of vertical side-armour. The sailing rig was removed in 1885 and replaced by pole masts with fighting tops. Her first captain, in 1881, was John Arbuthnot Fisher, later to be First Sea Lord. She was present at the bombardment of Alexandria at which her firing was both impressive and accurate, 88 rounds being fired at Ras-el-Tin, Mex and Pharos Forts. She spent long periods in reserve and as guardship in Portsmouth until 1903 when she was sold for scrap.

(T. Ferrers-Walker Collection)

HMS AJAX was built in Pembroke Dockyard between 1876 and 1883. She followed the general design of INFLEXIBLE but had less armour, was cheaper and built without a sailing rig from the outset. Her four 12.5-inch MLR guns each weighed 38 tons. She was said to combine all Inflexible's drawbacks and none of her virtues and was a poor sea boat, another example of cost-cutting producing a less than adequate ship. She was used as a Coastguard ship at Greenock from 1885 until 1891 when she was reduced to reserve at Chatham. She was broken up in 1904. *(T. Ferrers-Walker Collection)*

Concern about possible conflict with Russia in 1878 led to two warships being taken over for the Royal Navy. HMS BELLEISLE had been designed in Turkey for the Turkish Navy and was being built in the UK at the time of the crisis. She was originally rated as an 'armour-plated ram ship' and later as a second-class battleship. Note the ram bow and low superstructure. BELLEISLE was used as a Coastguard ship at Kingston in Ireland for fourteen years, during which she seldom left her mooring. In 1900 she became the first armoured ship to be fitted out as a fleet target and was used for a number of trials to ascertain the damage caused by a variety of shells and torpedoes. She was sunk by gunfire in 1903 but subsequently raised and sold for scrap.

(T. Ferrers-Walker Collection)

Designed for the Turkish Government and built by Thames Ironworks between 1873 and 1880, HMS SUPERB was originally to have been the Turkish Ship HAMIDIEH but she was requisitioned for the Royal Navy in 1878. Based on HMS HERCULES, the design was already somewhat dated when she was completed but she served in the Mediterranean Fleet from 1880 to 1887. She fired 310 shells from her main battery during the siege of Alexandria. After her return to the UK she underwent a modernisation at Chatham which included the removal of her sailing rig. After service as guardship on the Clyde from 1891 she was reduced to reserve in 1894. In 1904 she became a hospital ship for dealing with infectious cases and was then laid up in the Kyles of Bute before being scrapped in 1906.

(T. Ferrers-Walker Collection)

HMS NEPTUNE, built by J & W Dudgeon of Millwall on the Thames, was the last British turret battleship to be constructed with a sailing rig. She was originally to have been the Brazilian INDEPENDENCIA but was purchased for the Royal Navy during the 'Russian war scare' in 1878 and completed at Portsmouth Dockyard in 1882. Commissioned for the Channel Fleet in 1883, she subsequently served in the Mediterranean from 1885 and then returned to Portsmouth to have her sailing rig removed in 1886. She was guardship at Holyhead from 1887 to 1893 and then returned to reserve at Portsmouth. She was subsequently sold for scrap and, when being towed out of Portsmouth Harbour on 23 October 1903 she broke lose from her tugs, rammed and very nearly sank HMS VICTORY.

(T. Ferrers-Walker Collection)

HMS EDINBURGH was built in Pembroke Dockyard between 1879 and 1887 and was the first British warship in which steel, rather than iron, was used for the construction of the hull. Built from the outset without a sailing rig, she was regarded as a 'sound' ship, achieving 16 knots from 6,808 hp on trials. The photograph shows her in immaculate condition for the 1887 Jubilee Review at Portsmouth. She subsequently served in the Mediterranean Fleet until 1894 and then became guardship first at Hull, then Queensferry. She became Flagship of the Nore Command in 1897 and then a tender to HMS WILDFIRE at Sheerness in 1899, used as a gunnery training ship. She changed roles in 1908, becoming a gunnery target, fitted with modern armour plates used to test the impact of Armour-Piercing (AP) shells striking at oblique angles. She was broken up on completion of the trials.

(T. Ferrers-Walker Collection)

HMS CONQUEROR was designed as a modified version of an earlier battleship, HMS RUPERT, with improvements suggested by that ship's captain. She was built at Chatham Dockyard and completed in 1886 with an armament of two 12-inch BL 25 calibre guns in a single turret forward. The design was heavily criticised and considered unfit for anything other than gunnery practice in inshore waters but she did take part in the Jubilee Review in 1887. After that she became a tender to HMS CAMBRIDGE, the gunnery school at Devonport. *(T. Ferrers-Walker Collection)*

HMS CONQUEROR never went out of sight of land apart from occasional use in annual fleet mobilisations between 1888 and 1894. She is seen here in the last days of her use as a gunnery training ship painted grey. She was laid up at Rothesay in 1905 and sold for scrap in 1907.

(T. Ferrers-Walker Collection)

HMS COLLINGWOOD introduced a new, more effective, era of battleship design. She was built at Pembroke Dockyard, completed in 1887 and was the first British battleship to have guns mounted in barbettes although they were not enclosed in turrets. Her huge coal bunkerage gave her a higher endurance than any other warship at the time, 7,000 miles at 10 knots. She was a 'wet' ship in a head sea but capable of making over 16 knots. Despite this, her guns were easier to work than in previous classes because they were mounted higher. After the 1887 Jubilee Review she was placed in reserve before joining the Mediterranean Fleet in 1889. From 1897 to 1903 she was guardship at Bantry after which she reduced to reserve in Devonport before being laid up in East Kyle. She was sold for scrap in 1909. *(T. Ferrers-Walker Collection)*

HMS WARSPITE and her sister-ship IMPERIEUSE were regarded by most officers as complete failures. They were lightly armed with four 9.2-inch guns, one forward, one aft and one on each beam but capable of 16 knots with an endurance of 5,500 miles at 10 knots. WARSPITE was the flagship of the Pacific Squadron from 1890 to 1893 and again from 1899 to 1902 with periods in reserve and as guardship at Queenstown in between. She returned to reserve at Chatham in 1902 and was scrapped in 1905.

(T. Ferrers-Walker Collection)

A lack of suitable slipways in the Royal Dockyards in 1882 led to the contract for HMS BENBOW being given to Thames Iron-works. She was armed with two massive 16.25-inch BL guns mounted on barbettes, one forward and one aft. Each gun weighed over 110 tons and they were, for a time, the biggest guns afloat. They were intended to 'smash' an enemy warship with a single hit. She served in the Mediterranean Fleet from 1888 to 1891 and then went into reserve at Chatham. Guard ship at Greenock between 1894 and 1904, she later went into un-maintained reserve at Devonport and was sold for scrap in 1909.

(T. Ferrers-Walker Collection)

HMS SANS PAREIL and her sister-ship VICTORIA were the last single-turret battleships in the Royal Navy but were the first to be fitted with triple-expansion engines which gave them a speed of over 17 knots on 14,000 hp with forced-draught. SANS PAREIL was built by Thames Ironworks but commissioned at Chatham in 1891 after a three year delay in construction waiting for the delivery of her two 16.25-inch guns. She served in the Mediterranean Fleet from 1892 to 1895. After that she became a tender to HMS WILDFIRE at Sheerness and then part of the Reserve Fleet from 1898. She is seen here painted grey during the 1904 fleet manoeuvres for which she was brought out of reserve. She was sold for scrap in 1907.

(T. Ferrers-Walker Collection)

HMS VICTORIA flying the flag of Admiral Sir George Tryon, Commander-in-Chief Mediterranean Fleet. She was lost with him and 22 officers and 336 men on 22 June 1893 when rammed by HMS CAMPERDOWN during manoeuvres in the eastern Mediterranean. She had commissioned in 1890 and was never a 'lucky' ship. On 29 January 1892 she ran aground at Snipe Point, Platea and was not re-floated until 4 February after being lightened by over 1,000 tons. She was hauled off by EDINBURGH and DREADNOUGHT. During subsequent repairs in Malta she was the first ship to enter the Hamilton dry dock.

(T. Ferrers-Walker Collection)

HMS TRAFALGAR was built in Portsmouth Dockyard and completed in 1890. She had turrets fore and aft each with two 13.5-inch BL guns and mounted a secondary battery of 4.7-inch quick-firing guns intended for use against torpedo-boats. Dockyard re-organisation led to a shortened building time of only three and a half years, despite delays waiting for delivery of the heavy guns. She was commissioned in 1890 and served in the Mediterranean Fleet until returning to Portsmouth in 1897 to become the port guard ship. In 1902 she reduced to reserve first at Portsmouth, then Devonport and finally Sheerness before being sold for scrap in 1911.

(T. Ferrers-Walker Collection)

HMS REPULSE in her original black, white and buff paint scheme before the general adoption of grey in 1903. She first commissioned in 1894 having been built at Pembroke Dockyard in only four years. In addition to the heavy guns, her armament included seven torpedo tubes, two of which were below the waterline in the bow, four above water on the beam and one above water at the stern. She served in the Channel Fleet until 1902 followed by a brief spell with the Mediterranean Fleet until 1904. After a long period in reserve in Chatham, and Devonport she was laid up in Motherbank in the Solent 1910 and sold for scrap in 1911.

(T. Ferrers-Walker Collection)

HMS ROYAL OAK in 1906 in the newly standardised grey paint scheme. She was built at Laird's Yard at Birkenhead and spent two years after completion in 1894 in the reserve fleet at Portsmouth. The 13.5-inch guns had to be trained fore and aft to be loaded from fixed trunks built into the barbettes. She was commissioned for the Particular Service Squadron in 1896 and then joined the Mediterranean Fleet from 1897 to 1902. She was modernised with casemates for the main armament at Chatham Dockyard in 1902 and served in the Home Fleet from 1903 to 1905. After a small-arms magazine explosion on 11 May 1905 she spent the remainder of her life in reserve at decreasing levels of readiness before being sold for scrap in 1913.

(T. Ferrers-Walker Collection)

HMS ROYAL SOVEREIGN was built in Portsmouth Dockyard between 1889 and 1892 and commissioned for service as the flagship of the Channel Fleet on completion, attending the ceremonial opening of the Kiel Canal in 1895. With all her coal bunkers full she could carry 1,490 tons giving an endurance of 5,000 miles at 10 knots. She served in the Mediterranean Fleet from 1897 to 1902, suffering an accidental explosion of a 6-inch gun in 1901 that killed 6 and wounded 19 sailors. She was refitted with casemates for the main armament in 1903 after which she spent the rest of her life in reserve before being sold out of service in 1913.

(T. Ferrers-Walker Collection)

HMS REVENGE in grey paint after 1903. She was built by Palmer's Yard and spent two years after completion in reserve. In 1896 she commissioned for the Mediterranean Fleet before paying off into reserve again in 1900. After a period as a gunnery training ship she was modernised at Chatham Dockyard in 1902. On 7 January 1912 she collided with HMS ORION in Portsmouth, taking in a considerable amount of water, but was subsequently repaired and resumed duty as a gunnery training ship. Laid up at Motherbank in 1913 but not scrapped before the outbreak of war, she was renamed HMS RE-DOUBTABLE in 1914 and commissioned for bombardment operations off the Belgian coast. In 1918 she became a tender to HMS VICTORY and in November 1919 was sold for scrap. *(Ken Kelly Collection)*

HMS HOOD was the last British battleship to be built with a low freeboard and main guns in simple turrets rather than bar-bettes. She proved inferior to the Royal Sovereign class in every way, despite her similar armament. Built in Chatham Dockyard between 1889 and 1893, she served in the Mediterranean Fleet on completion. In 1900 she became guardship at Pembroke Dockyard and then joined the Home Fleet in 1903. She paid off in 1904 and spent some years in reserve at decreasing states of readiness. By 1911 she was in un-maintained reserve in Portsmouth but was brought forward for use as a target for torpedo trials. In 1914 she was sunk as a block-ship in the southern entrance to Portland Harbour where her remains still lie.

(T. Ferrers-Walker Collection)

HMS BARFLEUR represented an attempt to reduce the cost of construction by building 'second-class' battleships capable of a limited range of tasks. The four 10-inch guns fired 500lb shells and were in armoured gun-shields mounted on barbettes which were, for the first time, circular rather than 'pear-shaped'. The guns were electrically trained and could move from 7 degrees depression to 35 degrees elevation in 14 seconds but were hand-loaded. She was built by Chatham Dockyard and commissioned in 1894 for the Mediterranean Fleet. From 1898 to 1902 she was flagship of the China Station, coming home for modernisation at Devonport Dockyard between 1902 and 1904. She took part in the 1904 fleet manoeuvres and then paid off into reserve. In 1909 she was laid up at Motherbank and then scrapped a year later. *(T. Ferrers-Walker Collection)*

HMS RENOWN represented an improved 'second class' design but had armour made of steel and the four 10-inch guns were hydraulically trained. She was built at Pembroke Dockyard between 1893 and 1897, acted as flagship at the Jubilee Review in that year and then became Vice Admiral Sir John Fisher's Flagship on the North America and West Indies Station until 1899, moving with him when he assumed command of the Mediterranean Fleet until 1902. He was impressed by her speed and fighting power and it is arguable that he conceived the idea of the battle-cruiser while flying his flag in her. She conveyed Their Royal Highnesses The Prince and Princess of Wales to India in 1905 and was reduced to reserve in 1906. After service as a tender to HMS VICTORY and as a stokers' training ship she was laid up at Motherbank in 1913 and sold for scrap in 1914.

(T. Ferrers-Walker Collection)

HMS MAGNIFICENT was one of the nine units of the Majestic class, outstanding ships which were effectively first-class developments of RENOWN. They were coal-fired with a bunker capacity for 1,900 tons but this was supplemented after modernisation with 400 tons of furnace fuel oil to give more efficient combustion. She was built in Chatham Dockyard between 1893 and 1895 and served with the Channel and Atlantic Fleets from completion until 1907 and then the Home Fleet at various states of readiness. From 1911 she served as a gunnery training ship at Devonport and grounded in fog near Cawsand Pier on 16 June 1913. Her turrets were removed for use in monitors in 1915 and she was later used first as a troopship and then as an ammunition store at Rosyth until 1919. She was sold for scrap in 1921. *(T. Ferrers-Walker Collection)*

HMS HANNIBAL at anchor with funnel markings showing that the photograph was taken in 1911. The two massive turrets, mounted on barbettes, each contained two 12-inch wire-wound guns of 35 calibres which weighed 46 tons. They fired an 860lb shell capable of penetrating an iron plate 33 inches thick at 1,000 yards. With no central fire-control system and guns aimed by individual gun-layers, this was considered to be a viable fighting range when she was built. In 1914 she became the guardship in the Humber Estuary and later at Scapa Flow. Her main turrets were removed in 1915 to be fitted to monitors and she was then used as a troop transport. She was sold for scrap in 1920. *(Ken Kelly Collection)*

A grey-painted HMS MARS in 1903, serving with the Channel Fleet. She was built at Laird's Yard and completed in 1897. On trials she achieved 10,159 hp giving a speed of 15.9 knots. When modernised in 1905 she was fitted with oil sprayers to augment the performance of her coal-fired boilers. After a period in reserve she served in the Channel Fleet in 1907 and then joined one of the lower-readiness divisions of the Home Fleet until 1912. After 1914 her guns and turrets were removed for use in monitors and she was used as a troop transport in the Gallipoli Campaign, taking part in the evacuations from ANZAC Cove and Cape Helles. She returned to the UK for use as a depot ship at Invergordon before being sold for scrap in 1921.

(T. Ferrers-Walker Collection)

HMS PRINCE GEORGE in 1905 after being damaged in a collision with the German cruiser FREIDRICH KARL, an incident for which blame was attributed to the German ship. She served in the Channel Fleet from 1896 to 1903 when she collided with HMS HANNIBAL. After repairs, she served in the Portsmouth Division of the Home Fleet, breaking loose from her moorings in 1911 and being badly damaged in a collision with HMS SHANNON. Repaired again she went into reserve at Devonport but re-commissioned as the Flagship of 7 BS in 1914, after which she was fitted as a 'mine-bumper' and took part on the naval assault on the Dardanelles narrows in March 1915. Subsequently used for bombardment operations in support of the land campaign, she was hit by shore batteries on 2 May and repaired in Malta. Later hit by a torpedo that failed to explode while covering the evacuation from Cape Helles in 1916. After returning to the UK she was used as an auxiliary sick-bay and depot ship for destroyers at Chatham before being sold for scrap in 1921. *(Ken Kelly Collection)*

HMS GLORY in 1905. She was an improved Majestic class vessel with the same main armament of four 12-inch 35 calibre guns and was built by Lairds and floated out of dry dock rather than launched in 1899. Commissioned in 1900 she
served on the China Station and both the Channel and Mediterranean Fleets before reducing to reserve in 1909. In 1914
she re-commissioned for 8 BS and escorted the first Canadian troop convoy to the UK in October. She subsequently became the flagship of the North America and West Indies Station and then guard ship of the Suez Canal in 1916. Later in
1916 she deployed to Murmansk and remained there until returning to the UK in 1919. Re-named HMS CRESCENT in
1919, she was used as a depot ship at Rosyth until she was sold for scrap in 1922. *(T. Ferrers-Walker Collection)*

HMS VENGEANCE in 1909. She was the first British battleship to be built, engined, armed and armoured by a single firm, Vickers at Barrow in Furness. She was also one of the first to be fitted with water-tube boilers. Completed in 1902 she served on the China Station and with the Channel and Home Fleets before becoming a gunnery training ship in 1909. She was fitted with a Siemens's fire control system in 1913 and joined 8 BS for war service in 1914. In 1915 she was the Flagship of Admiral de Robeck and took part in both the February and March bombardments of the Dardanelles. She later became the Egypt guardship until 1917 when she returned to Devonport for use as a floating ordnance depot. Sold for scrap in 1921.

(Ken Kelly Collection)

HMS IRRESISTIBLE was built at Chatham Dockyard and was one of the first battleships to cost more than £1 million. She was completed in 1902 and served in the Mediterranean Fleet until 1908. She carried 80 rounds for each of her four 12-inch 40 calibre guns. On 3 March 1902 she collided with the SS CLIVE and had to be repaired in Malta. In 1906 she was fitted with an early form of centralised fire-control system and joined the Home Fleet with a nucleus crew. In 1914 she was brought forward for 5 BS and used for patrols in the English Channel. In 1915 she deployed to the eastern Mediterranean and took part in both the February and March assaults on the Dardanelles. During the latter, on 18 March 1915, she was mined at 1615 and abandoned but remained afloat to be carried by the tide into the range of the narrows forts which finally sank her with gunfire at about 1930.

(T. Ferrers-Walker Collection)

HMS IMPLACABLE shortly after completion in her original paint scheme. She was built in Devonport Dockyard and served with the Mediterranean Fleet from 1904 to 1908, being fitted with centralised fire-control in 1906. After boiler explosions in 1905 and 1906 she was refitted for service with the Channel and Atlantic Fleets; reducing to a nucleus crew at the Nore in 1912. Re-commissioned for 5 BS in 1914 she deployed to the Dardanelles in March 1915 and covered the landings at Cape Helles on 25 April 1915. In May she was sent to the Adriatic to reinforce the Italian Fleet until returning to the UK for duty with the Northern Patrol in 1917. Sold for scrap in 1921. *(T. Ferrers-Walker Collection)*

HMS QUEEN in 1909. She was built in Devonport Dockyard and completed in 1904, after which she served in the Mediterranean and Atlantic Fleets until 1910; flagship of the former between1907 and 1908. She was flagship of one of the reserve divisions of the Home Fleet from 1912 and re-commissioned for 5 BS in 1914. Ordered to the Dardanelles in 1915, she covered the landings at ANZAC Cove on 25 April 1915. Later, she deployed to the Adriatic with other British battleships to strengthen the Italian Fleet. She was the guardship at Taranto until 1918 after which she returned to the UK and was sold for scrap in 1920.

(T. Ferrers-Walker Collection)

HMS LONDON was built in Portsmouth Dockyard and completed in 1902. She was flagship at the Coronation Naval Review before service in the Mediterranean, Channel and Atlantic Fleets as flagship until 1912 when she joined the Home Fleet with a reduced complement. In May 1912 she was used for flying experiments with a take-off ramp built over the forecastle capable of launching a single aircraft. In 1914 she joined 5 BS in the Channel before being ordered to the eastern Mediterranean to replace ships lost in the Dardanelles campaign. She is seen here after her return to the UK in 1918 painted in an experimental disruptive scheme designed to confuse enemy range-finders. By then, her guns had been removed and she was fitted for use as a mine-layer. She was sold for scrap in 1920. *(Author's Collection)*

HMS EXMOUTH was one of six battleships of the Duncan class. She was built by Lairds, completed in 1903 and saw service with the Mediterranean, Home and Atlantic Fleets before 1913 when she became a gunnery training ship at Devonport. After 1914 she served in the Northern Patrol and in the Channel before proceeding to the Dardanelles in May 1915. She remained in the Eastern Mediterranean until 1917 when she returned to the UK and paid off into reserve. She was sold for scrap in 1920.

(Ken Kelly Collection)

HMS MONTAGU in 1906. Steam was produced by twenty-four Belleville boilers working at 300psi with a grate area of 1,375 square feet and a heating surface of 43,260 square feet. Two sets of triple-expansion steam engines produced 18,000 hp which gave 19 knots. She was built at Devonport Dockyard between 1899 and 1903 and served in the Mediterranean Fleet after completion and the Channel Fleet from 1905. On 30 May 1906 she hit Lundy Island in fog and became a constructive total loss. After the removal of useful items, she was scrapped in situ. *(T. Ferrers-Walker Collection)*

HMS HINDUSTAN was armed with four 12-inch 50 calibre, four 9.2-inch 45 calibre and ten 6-inch 50 calibre guns with 80, 150 and 200 rounds per gun respectively. The smaller guns were intended to overwhelm an opponent with a high volume of close-range fire. She was built on the Clyde and served with the Atlantic, Channel and Home Fleets. In 1914 she was serving in 3 BS with the Grand Fleet. After the German raid on Lowestoft, 3BS was based in the Thames Estuary from May 1916 to provide heavy cover well south of the main fleet in Scapa Flow. She was sold for scrap in 1921.

(T. Ferrers-Walker Collection)

HMS HIBERNIA in the early morning of 2 May 1912 near Portland, about to sail into Weymouth Bay to launch Naval Aircraft Number 2, from the take-off platform rigged over the forecastle. In the previous January, Commander Charles R Samson RN had taken off from a similar platform rigged on her sister-ship HMS AFRICA while she was moored in Sheerness and on this day he took off from HIBERNIA while she was under way and steaming at 10½ knots into a slight natural wind several miles off-shore, the first time an aircraft had taken off from a moving ship. Before 1914 she served with the Channel, Atlantic and Home Fleets and during the war she served with 3 BS in the Grand Fleet until November 1915 when she became the Flagship of Admiral Freemantle in the eastern Mediterranean. In 1919 she de-commissioned for use as an accommodation ship at the Nore and in 1921 she was broken up for scrap in Germany.   (T. Ferrers-Walker Collection)

HMS ZEALANDIA was built in Portsmouth Dockyard between 1903 and 1905 and was originally named NEW ZEALAND. Her name was changed in December 1911 to free the original for the battle-cruiser presented to the RN by the government and people of New Zealand. She served in the Atlantic, Channel and Home Fleets from completion until 1912 After a short spell in the Mediterranean she joined 3 BS in 1914 and then saw service in the Dardanelles Campaign. She was used as an accommodation ship at Portsmouth in 1919 and was broken up for scrap in Germany in 1921.

(Syd Goodman Collection)

In December 1903 the Admiralty purchased two lightweight battleships under construction for Chile in British shipyards to prevent them being bought by Russia. The former LIBERTAD was re-named HMS TRIUMPH and she served in the Channel and Mediterranean Fleets until 1912 and then the China Station where she reduced to reserve in 1913. In 1914 she was re-commissioned with men from the river gunboats and was present at the capture of the German colony of Tsingtao by the Japanese. She re-deployed to the eastern Mediterranean and was part of the force that attacked the forts in the Dardanelles in February and March 1915 and covered the landings at ANZAC Cove with gunfire. On 25 May 1915 she was torpedoed by U-21, despite having her anti-torpedo nets down, and capsized and sank ten minutes later. The destroyer HMS CHELMER rescued over 500 of her officers and men from the water, 3 officers and 70 men were lost. *(Author's Collection)*

HMS SWIFTSURE, originally named CONSTITUTION, was purchased from Chile. She was built at Elswick on Tyne and served with the Home, Channel and Mediterranean Fleets before becoming flagship of the East Indies Fleet in 1913. In 1914 she escorted Indian troopships as far as Aden and then became flagship of the force tasked with protecting Egypt and the Suez Canal. She bombarded Turkish positions at Kantara and joined the fleet off the Dardanelles in March 1915, covering the landings at both Cape Helles and Suvla Bay. After the evacuation she returned to the UK to become an accommodation 'overflow' ship at Chatham. She was stripped of useful equipment in 1919 and used as a target in gunnery trials after which she was scrapped in 1920.

(T. Ferrers-Walker Collection)

HMS LORD NELSON was one of the last British battleships to be built with a mixed armament of heavy guns, four 12-inch 80 calibre and ten 9.2-inch 50 calibre. She was built by Palmers and completed in 1908, spending a year in reserve before joining the Home Fleet in 1909. In 1914 she was the flagship of the Channel Fleet and covered the passage of the BEF to France in August. In February 1915 she deployed to the Dardanelles and took part in operations in the eastern Mediterranean, Adriatic and Black Sea until 1919 when she paid off in the UK. She was sold for scrap in 1920.

(Syd Goodman Collection)

HMS AGAMEMNON was built by Beardmore on the Clyde. Although her design had been overtaken by the revolutionary HMS DREADNOUGHT, she was still a very powerful ship by international standards and served in the Home Fleet from 1908 and 5 BS with the Channel Fleet in 1914. In 1915 she deployed to the Dardanelles and fought throughout the campaign there being hit by over fifty enemy projectiles including a 14-inch stone shot. On 5 May 1916 she shot down Zeppelin L-85 off Salonika and remained in the area to guard against a possible break-out by the Turkish-manned GOEBEN. The terms of the Allied Armistice with Turkey were signed on board in 1918, after which she returned to Chatham in February 1919.

(Ken Kelly Collection)

HMS AGAMEMNON sailing from Portsmouth after her conversion to a radio-controlled target ship in 1923. All her guns were removed and she was steamed to the operating area by a skeleton crew who were then taken off by a destroyer from which the ship was controlled while she was under fire. After the shoot, the crew re-boarded her to resume manual control and took her back into port. AGAMEMNON was used in both home and Mediterranean waters before being sold for scrap in 1926.

(T. Ferrers-Walker Collection)

HMS DREADNOUGHT revolutionised battleship design and made all her predecessors obsolescent. She was built in Portsmouth Dockyard in a year and a day, a considerable amount of time being saved by using the 12-inch guns, turrets and spares ordered for the two Lord Nelsons. She introduced a standard all-big-gun armament of ten 12-inch 45 calibre guns and was the first large warship to have steam turbines, giving her a speed of 21 knots, making her the fastest battleship afloat for a time. There were defects in the design; having a spotting top on the fore mast aft of the foremost funnel was never a good idea and left those manning it suffering from heat exhaustion and smoke inhalation. Such was her advance over previous ships, however, that all subsequent battleships of every navy were known as 'Dreadnoughts'.

(T. Ferrers-Walker Collection)

HMS DREADNOUGHT's 12-inch guns were capable of long-range fire against targets that were beyond the gun-crews' horizon, hence the need for the spotting top, high on the fore mast, to observe the fall of shot; the tripod mast was intended to keep it as rigid as possible so that optical instruments did not vibrate. The 12-pdr guns were intended for use against torpedo-boats and the hull included 5,000 tons of steel armour plate. After sea trials she became flagship of the Home Fleet from 1907 to 1912. She was in 4 BS with the Grand Fleet in 1914 and on 18 March 1915 she sighted, rammed and sank U-29 (which had earlier sunk the cruisers ABOUKIR, CRESSY and HOGUE) about fifty miles south east of the Pentland Firth. She was re-fitting at the time of Jutland and was transferred from the Grand Fleet to become the flagship 3 BS at Sheerness in July 1916. She reduced to reserve at Rosyth in 1919 and was sold for scrap in 1922. *(Ken Kelly Collection)*

HMS INFLEXIBLE was one of the first battle-cruisers. She was built on Clydebank and her armament included eight 12-inch 45 calibre guns. She had thirty-one Yarrow boilers, Parsons geared turbines, high freeboard to ensure high speed in the open sea and tall masts which gave long W/T range. She is seen here attending the Hudson/Fulton celebrations at New York as flagship of Admiral of the Fleet Sir Edward Seymour in 1909. From 1912 she was the flagship of the C-in-C Mediterranean Fleet and in 1914 returned to the UK before taking part in the Battle of the Falkland Islands, exactly the kind of action she was designed for, sinking the German cruisers SCHARNHORST and GNEISENAU without receiving any damage. In 1915 she joined the force off the Dardanelles as Admiral Carden's Flagship. During the attempt to force the narrows on 18 March she was mined and took in 2,000 tons of water, subsequently being repaired at Gibraltar before joining the Battle-Cruiser Force of the Grand Fleet in June 1915. She was at Jutland in 1916, paid off into un-maintained reserve at the Nore in 1919 and sold for scrap in 1922.

(Ken Kelly Collection)

HMS INDOMITABLE at Portland in 1909. A year earlier she conveyed HRH The Prince of Wales, later King George V, to Quebec for its Tercentenary Celebrations. During the passage he spent a watch as a stoker to see the conditions under which the men worked. In 1914 she was with 2 BCS with INFLEXIBLE in the Mediterranean Fleet, hunted the GOEBEN and BRESLAU and joined the Dardanelles task force. She joined the Battle-Cruiser Force of the Grand Fleet in 1915 and fought at Dogger Bank, after which she towed the damaged LION home. She formed part of 3 BCS at Jutland without suffering damage or casualties; later she moved to 2 BCS and remained in it until 1919. She paid off in 1920 and was sold for scrap in 1922.

(T. Ferrers-Walker Collection)

HMS SUPERB was built at Elswick and completed in 1909 as an 'improved Dreadnought' with 4-inch rather than 12-pdr guns to counter torpedo-boats. She is seen here with 1 BS of the Grand Fleet in 1914 having served with the Home Fleet initially after completion. Before Jutland she became flagship of 4 BS and suffered no damage or casualties in the battle. In 1918 she joined the Mediterranean Fleet and led the Allied Fleet through the Dardanelles after the surrender of Turkey. She became a turret drill ship after returning to the UK in 1919 and then a gunnery target before being discarded under the terms of the Washington Naval Treaty and scrapped in 1922. *(Syd Goodman Collection)*

HMS TEMERAIRE joined the Home Fleet in 1909 and was with 4 BS of the Grand Fleet in 1914. She fought at Jutland in 1916 and transferred to the Mediterranean Fleet in 1918. In 1919, after returning to the UK, she became a training ship for officer cadets and is seen here in that role in 1920. She was withdrawn from service and scrapped under the terms of the Washington Naval Treaty in 1922. *(T. Ferrers-Walker Collection)*

HMS ST VINCENT represented a further improvement in battleship design and is seen here in 1913. She was built in Portsmouth Dockyard and completed in 1910 armed with ten 12-inch 50 calibre and twenty 4-inch 50 calibre guns. 2,800 tons of coal and 940 tons of oil gave an endurance of 6,900 miles at 10 knots. The rise in big gun calibres from 45 to 50 was introduced to increase the guns' battle range and give better armour-piercing effect; muzzle velocity being increased from 2,850 fps to 3,010 fps with the same shells. The net gain was increased penetration - the equivalent to about half an inch of armour at 3,000 yards. She joined the Home Fleet on completion in 1910 and 1 BS of the Grand Fleet in 1914. After Jutland she transferred to 4 BS and remained with it until 1919 when she became a gunnery training ship at Portsmouth. Discarded under the terms of the Washington Naval treaty, she was broken up in 1922.   *(T. Ferrers-Walker Collection)*

HMS VANGUARD was built by Vickers and completed in 1910; on trials she achieved 25,800 hp and 22 knots, exceeding her design speed. She served with the Home Fleet from 1910 and was with 1 BS of the Grand Fleet in 1914. She fought at Jutland without damage or casualties but on 9 July 1917 she was destroyed by an internal explosion at Scapa Flow, believed to have been caused by incorrectly stowed, faulty cordite, with the loss of 804 men.   *(Author's Collection)*

HMS NEPTUNE was the first British battleship to have a superimposed turret, visible here in 'X' position, and to be able to train all its main armament on either beam. She was built at Portsmouth Dockyard and completed in 1911. 2,710 tons of coal and 790 tons of oil gave her an endurance of 6,330 miles at 10 knots. She commissioned as flagship of the C-in-C Home Fleet in 1911 and formed part of 1 BS Grand Fleet in 1914. She fought at Jutland and then transferred to 4 BS in 1917 before being reduced to reserve in 1919 and discarded under the terms of the Washington Treaty in 1922.

(T. Ferrers-Walker Collection)

HMS INDEFATIGABLE was an improved battle-cruiser design and served with 1 BCS in 1913 and 2 BCS in the Mediterranean in 1914 when she took part in the unsuccessful hunt for GOEBEN and BRESLAU. After moving to the eastern Mediterranean she bombarded Cape Helles on 3 November 1914 and was Admiral Carden's Flagship until January 1915 when she was re-fitted at Malta. She subsequently joined 2 BCS in the Battle Cruiser Fleet and was sunk at 1605 on 31 May 1916 during the Battle of Jutland.

(T. Ferrers-Walker Collection)

HMAS AUSTRALIA was a unit of the Indefatigable class ordered by the Australian Government for the Royal Australian Navy to act as flagship of a 'fleet unit' with cruisers, destroyers and submarines. She was built by John Brown & Co of Clydebank between 1910 and 1913 and achieved 26.9 knots on trials. She proceeded to Australia on completion and in 1914 was flagship of an Australian force that operated against German possessions in the Pacific. In 1915 she returned to the UK and became the flagship of 2 BCS. On 22 April 1916 she collided with HMS NEW ZEALAND in fog and missed Jutland because of the subsequent repairs. She spent the remainder of the war as flagship of 2 BCS. *(T. Ferrers-Walker Collection)*

HMAS AUSTRALIA returned to Sydney on 15 June 1919 and paid off into reserve on 12 December 1921 when she was discarded under the terms of the Washington Naval Treaty. She was not scrapped but, after being stripped of useful material, was towed out to sea and sunk with honours off Sydney Head. She is seen here rolling to port with her white ensign still flying on the quarterdeck.

(Ferrers-Walker Collection)

HMS NEW ZEALAND was paid for by the people of New Zealand and presented by them to the Royal Navy (the Royal New Zealand Navy was not created until 1942). A proportion of her ship's company came from New Zealand. She was built by Fairfield and, after completion, sailed on a world cruise visiting Dominions and Colonies as tangible evidence of Imperial co-operation on defence. She joined the Battle-Cruiser Force in 1913 and, as part of 1 BCS in 1914, fought at Dogger Bank, replacing HMS LION which was damaged in action. At Jutland she was hit on 'X' turret but suffered no casualties, the popular belief being that she could come to no harm while the captain wore a Maori 'apron' in action. From late 1916 to 1919 she served with 2 BCS and then conveyed Admiral Sir John Jellicoe on a tour of the Pacific when he drew up his scheme for Imperial defence and future naval forces in the region. She was discarded under the terms of the Washington Naval Treaty and scrapped in 1922.

(T. Ferrers-Walker Collection)

HMS COLOSSUS and other units of the Grand Fleet anchored off Lyness Naval base in Scapa Flow. Her side turrets were staggered to allow all ten 12-inch guns to fire on either beam, unlike the earlier Dreadnoughts. She was built by Scotts and completed in 1911, serving in the Home Fleet on completion and with 1 BS Grand Fleet in 1914. At Jutland she was flagship of 1 BS and was the only battleship in the Grand Fleet to be hit by enemy gunfire, suffering five casualties. In 1919 she became a static training ship for cadets at Devonport and was painted for a time in the old Victorian black, white and buff scheme. She was sold for scrap in 1920. *(Ken Kelly Collection)*

HMS HERCULES could be distinguished from her sister-ship COLOSSUS by the shields on her 4-inch guns and the single white band seen here on her after funnel. On completion in 1911 she became flagship of the Second Division, Home Fleet. In 1913 she became flagship of 2 BS and in 1914 she formed part of 1 BS. She fought at Jutland and later became flagship of 4 BS. After the Armistice in 1918 she carried the Allied Naval Commission to Kiel. She paid off in 1919 and was sold for scrap in 1920.

(T. Ferrers-Walker Collection)

HMS ORION introduced the new 13.5-inch 45 calibre gun in five twin turrets on the centreline with super-firing mountings in 'B' and 'X' positions. The 12-inch gun fitted in earlier battleships fired an 850lb shell and had reached the limit of development. The new gun was more accurate, capable of firing to a greater range, albeit with a need for greater elevation, and fired a 1,259lb projectile. Built at Portsmouth Dockyard, she commissioned in 1912 and later became flagship of 2 BS. She fought at Jutland and continued in the same BS throughout the war. She was discarded and sold for scrap in 1922.

(Ken Kelly Collection)

HMS CONQUEROR at anchor. On her initial sea trials she steamed at over 22 knots and was regarded as a good sea-boat once her bilge-keels were enlarged. She was built by Beardmore on Clydebank and her main armoured belt was 12-inches thick, tapering to 8-inches at the ends and the turret faces were 11-inches thick. She had armoured decks ranging from 4-inches to 1-inch and 1½-inches around the magazines. Her torpedo nets in the stowed position are clearly visible in this view, as is the super-firing 'B' turret. She spent her entire career in 2 BS until she was discarded under the terms of the Washington Naval Treaty in 1922.

(T. Ferrers-Walker Collection)

HMS THUNDERER was the last battleship to be built on the Thames and took just over two years to build. Her entire operational career from 1912, which included the Battle of Jutland in 1916, was spent in 2 BS with the Grand Fleet. She saw post-war service as a cadet training ship until she was sold for scrap in 1926.　　　　　　　　　　　*(Author's Collection)*

The first test of the new 'giant floating dock' in Portsmouth involved lifting HMS MONARCH. The evolution took five hours and the ship is seen here 'high and dry'. She spent her whole operational life from 1912 to 1924 in 2 BS and saw action at Jutland. She was discarded under the terms of the Washington Naval Treaty and sunk as a target on 20 January 1925. This involved being attacked by aircraft in the morning, cruisers in the afternoon and by battleships using searchlights at night. After all that, she was still afloat when the shooting ended and she had to be sunk by close-range, deliberate gunfire from HMS REVENGE. The difficulty experienced in sinking her showed what well designed and constructed ships the Orions were.
(Syd GoodmanCollection)

The First Battle-Cruiser Squadron photographed in 1922. The original caption expressed sadness that HM Ships LION and PRINCESS ROYAL were soon to be discarded under the terms of the Washington Naval Treaty. *(Ken Kelly Collection)*

HMS LION was the first capital ship to cost over £2 million. Built at Devonport Dockyard, she had forty-two Yarrow boilers which worked at 235psi and Parsons steam turbines developing 73,800 hp on four shafts to achieve a speed of 27 knots. She is seen here in 1918 with a Sopwith 2F.1 Camel on the platform over the after turret; a Sopwith 1½ Strutter would have been carried on the centre turret during operations. She became Admiral David Beatty's Flagship in 1 BCS in 1913 and remained the Flagship of the Battle Cruiser Fleet throughout the war, seeing action at Heligoland, Dogger Bank and Jutland, receiving extensive damage in the last two. At Jutland an enemy shell hit the roof of 'Q' turret and set fire to cordite charges in the lower cages. The Officer of the Turret, Major F Harvey RMLI gave the order to close the magazine doors and flood it before he died. Had he not done so the ship would have blown up like others on the day and he was posthumously awarded the VC for his gallant action. After the war LION continued to serve as the Flagship of 1 BCS in the Atlantic Fleet until 1923 when she was withdrawn from service under the terms of the Washington Naval Treaty. She was broken up for scrap in 1924 at Jarrow.

(T. Ferrers-Walker Collection)

HMS PRINCESS ROYAL in 1918; note the canvas screen rigged as a hangar to protect the aircraft on 'Y' turret and the Sop-with 2F.1 on 'Q' turret. She fought at Heligoland Bight in 1914, Dogger Bank in 1915 and Jutland in 1916 and served in 1 BCS from 1913 to 1923. She was damaged at Jutland with numerous fires which were difficult to extinguish because of rup-tured fire mains and the loss of lighting circuits. She was discarded under the terms of the Washington Treaty and was sold for scrap in 1926.

(T. Ferrers-Walker Collection)

HMS KING GEORGE V in March 1913 shortly after her completion with a large, circular control top with a director for the main armament at the top of the tripod fore mast. She was built in Portsmouth Dockyard and commissioned as the flagship of the Home Fleet in 1912. In 1914 she became the flagship of 2 BS in the Grand Fleet and subsequently fought at Jutland. After the war, she served as flagship of the Mediterranean Fleet from 1919 to 1923 when she became a gunnery training ship in Devonport. She was sold for scrap in 1926. *(Author's Collection)*

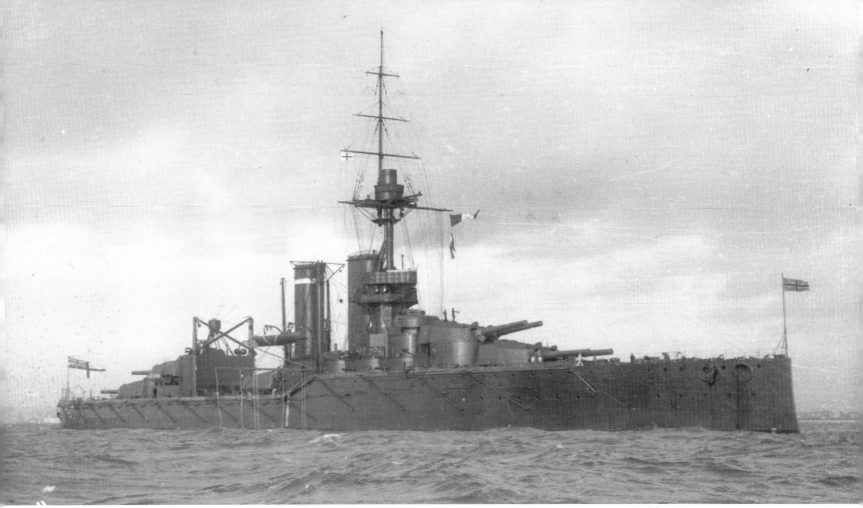

HMS AUDACIOUS had a short and unfortunate career. She was built by Lairds and commissioned for service in the Home Fleet in 1913. In 1914 she joined 2 BS in the Grand Fleet but on 27 October 1914 she was mined while on gunnery exercises off Lough Swilly (Ireland) and subsequently sank. Her loss showed that the thin longitudinal bulkheads in the engine rooms were inadequate to provide protection against damage caused by mines. The port engine room was completely flooded, another partially flooded and water continued to seep through bulkhead penetrations for pipes and cables for twelve hours. She finally sank after an internal explosion   *(T. Ferrers-Walker Collection)*

HMS AJAX was built by Scotts and spent the whole of World War 1 in 2 BS with the Grand Fleet, seeing action at Jutland in 1916. In 1919 she transferred to the Mediterranean Fleet and was one of a number of British battleships that saw action against the Bolsheviks in the Black Sea. She remained in the Mediterranean until 1924 when she returned to the UK and reduced to un-maintained reserve status at the Nore. She was sold for scrap in 1926. *(Syd Goodman Collection)*

HMS CENTURION collided with and sank the Italian SS DERNA while on contractor's sea trials on 9 December 1912 and repairs took until March 1913 when she joined the Home Fleet. She spent the whole war in 2 BS, fought at Jutland, joined the Mediterranean Fleet in 1919 and saw action against Bolsheviks in the Black Sea. She returned to Portsmouth in 1924 and paid off into reserve until 1926 when she was selected for conversion into a target ship to replace AGAMEMNON. She was used in the role until 1941 and is seen here in 1936. Her method of operation involved leaving harbour controlled in the ordinary way by her small ship's company but before firing commenced they transferred to the destroyer SHIKARI from which radio-control was then exercised while CENTURION was under fire. After the shoot she was re-boarded, examined to see that she was safe and steamed into harbour under manual control. *(T. Ferrers-Walker Collection)*

In 1942 HMS CENTURION was converted to a 'dummy battleship' intended to look like the new ANSON and deployed around the Cape to Bombay. She was subsequently used as a floating anti-aircraft battery in the Suez Canal until March 1944 when she returned to the UK. In June 1944 she was sunk as a block-ship to form part of the breakwater intended to protect the Mulberry Harbour after the Allied landings in Normandy. Her remains still lie there.

(T. Ferrers-Walker Collection)

HMS IRON DUKE served as Admiral Jellicoe's Grand Fleet flagship from 1914 to 1916. She was built in Portsmouth Dockyard with a main armament of ten 13.5-inch 45 calibre guns. When QUEEN ELIZABETH became Flagship in 1916 she joined 2 BS until 1919 when she deployed to the Mediterranean Fleet and saw action in the Black Sea. Between 1926 and 1929 she served in the Atlantic Fleet and in 1931 she was partially disarmed under the terms of the London Naval Treaty to become a gunnery and boys' training ship. 'B' and 'Y' turrets were removed together with her conning tower, belt armour and torpedo tubes. Boiler power was reduced to give a maximum speed no greater than 18 knots. In 1939 she moved to Scapa Flow for use as a local defence and depot ship. She was damaged by air attack on 17 October 1939 but continued in service. She was finally sold and broken up in 1946. *(Syd Goodman Collection)*

HMS MARLBOROUGH was built at Devonport Dockyard and completed in June 1914. She served with 1 BS between 1914 and 1919 and was torpedoed at Jutland but managed to return to port without assistance. Repairs on the Tyne took three months. She served with the Mediterranean Fleet from 1919 and was part of the force that operated against the Bolsheviks in the Black Sea. In 1926 she joined the Atlantic Fleet until 1929 when she was withdrawn from service under the terms of the Washington Naval Treaty. She was sold for scrap in 1932. *(Author's Collection)*

HMS BENBOW at Istanbul in 1922. She was built by Beardmore, became flagship of 4 BS with the Grand Fleet in 1914 and remained as such until 1919, having fought at Jutland. She transferred to the Mediterranean with other battleships in 1919 and saw action in the Black Sea against Bolsheviks. From 1926 to 1929 she served with the Atlantic Fleet before being discarded under the terms of the Washington Treaty. She was scrapped in 1931. *(Ken Kelly Collection)*

HMS TIGER was built by John Brown & Co on Clydebank and displaced 35,160 tons. Thirty-nine Babcock & Wilcox boilers worked at 235psi and her four shafts were driven by Brown Curtis steam turbines developing 105,000 hp which gave a maximum speed of 29 knots. She joined 1 BCS in October 1914 after a short work-up and saw action at Dogger Bank and Jutland. In the latter, she received 21 hits and lost 24 men killed and 34 wounded. Repairs were complete by 2 July. From 1919 to 1922 she served with the BCS of the Atlantic Fleet and was a sea-going gunnery training ship from 1924 to 1929, returning to the Atlantic Fleet again from 1929-31. She paid off at Devonport in 1931 and was scrapped in 1932.

(T. Ferrers-Walker Collection)

HMS ERIN was one of several battleships being built in British shipyards for foreign navies that were requisitioned by the Admiralty on the outbreak of war in 1914. Laid down as the Turkish RESHADIEH and completed in August 1914, her design and equipment were so close to British requirements that she was quickly absorbed into 2 BS of the Grand Fleet after a short work-up and needed few modifications. She fought at Jutland and became flagship of the Nore reserve in 1919. She was sold for scrap in 1921. *(Author's Collection)*

HMS CANADA was requisitioned in 1914. She was laid down as the ALMIRANTE LATORRE for Chile at Elswick and taken over, incomplete, in 1914. Renamed, she joined 4 BS of the Grand Fleet on completion in October 1915 and served with the squadron throughout the remainder of the war, seeing action at Jutland. She mounted ten 14-inch 45 calibre guns, the only British battleship at the time to mount them. Her less advanced sister-ship ALMIRANTE COCHRANE eventually emerged as the aircraft carrier HMS EAGLE and remained in service with the Royal Navy. After the war CANADA was re-fitted at Devonport, resumed her original name and was returned to the Chilean Navy in which she continued in active service until 1957. She was broken up in 1959.

(T. Ferrers-Walker Collection)

HMS QUEEN ELIZABETH incorporated a number of design improvements. She was the first fully oil-fired British battleship, first to achieve 24 knots and the first to mount 15-inch 42 calibre guns, eight of which were mounted in four turrets. She is seen here on 2 June 1915, six months after completion, during operations in the eastern Mediterranean. On one occasion, during the Dardanelles Campaign, she sank a Turkish transport ship by shooting over the peninsula and hit it with the third 15-inch round fired. From 1916 to 1919 she was Admiral Sir David Beatty's Grand Fleet flagship. The surrender of the German High Sea Fleet was signed in her in 1918. From 1919 to 1924 she was the flagship of the Atlantic Fleet.

(Author's Collection)

From 1924 to 1929 HMS QUEEN ELIZABETH served in the Mediterranean Fleet in her original configuration, retaining aircraft platforms on 'B' and 'X' turrets and is seen here in 1927. She was one of the Fleet's most valuable units and underwent a series of modernisations throughout her long life. She returned briefly to the Atlantic Fleet in 1929 and then returned to the Mediterranean Fleet again until 1937 when she paid off for complete reconstruction in Portsmouth.

(Syd Goodman Collection)

HMS QUEEN ELIZABETH photographed from HMS NELSON in Gibraltar in 1931. She had already undergone a number of modifications including the trunking of the two funnels into one. Note the armoured director-control tower with its range-finders on top of the conning tower aft of 'B' turret and the aircraft platform on 'B' turret roof.
(Ken Kelly Collection)

HMS QUEEN ELIZABETH off Trincomalee, photographed from the USS SARATOGA which was serving with the British Eastern Fleet at the time. By then ten twin 4.5-inch mountings had replaced the 6-inch guns to give a much improved anti-aircraft capability and a catapult, hangars and cranes fitted to operate Walrus aircraft. The new 'tower' bridge structure had both high and low-angle directors on top of it and there was an extensive outfit of radar sets. She served in the Home Fleet after re-commissioning, moving to the Mediterranean Fleet in May 1941. On 19 December 1941 she was damaged by Italian frogmen in Alexandria and repaired in a floating dock. She was refitted in the USA in 1942 and became flagship of the Eastern Fleet in 1944. She supported amphibious landings on Ramree Island in Burma in January 1945 and her Royal Marines, with others from cruisers, captured Cheduba Island. She covered the recapture of Rangoon in May 1945 and then returned to the UK in July. She paid off into reserve at Rosyth in August 1945 and was broken up for scrap in 1948.

(Author's Collection)

HMS BARHAM was built by John Brown on Clydebank and became flagship of 5 BS on completion in 1915. 5 BS formed part of the battle-cruiser fleet at Jutland and BARHAM was hit six times with the loss of 26 men killed and 37 wounded. She served with the Atlantic and Mediterranean Fleets from 1920 to 1929. Between 1930 and 1933 she was modernised and after that alternated between the Home and Mediterranean Fleets again. *(T. Ferrers-Walker Collection)*

HMS BARHAM in the late 1930s serving with the Mediterranean Fleet. The stripes on 'B' turret are red, white and blue and indicate service with the Neutrality Patrol during the Spanish Civil War. The single, trunked funnel seen here replaced the earlier two funnels in 1927. BARHAM served in the Home Fleet in 1939 and was torpedoed by U-30 off the Hebrides on 28 December. After repairs in Liverpool, she moved to the Mediterranean and fought at the Battle of Matapan in March 1941. She was hit by bombs during the evacuation of the army from Crete. On 25 November 1941 she was hit by three torpedoes from U-331 while searching for an enemy convoy between Crete and Cyrenaica. She capsized and blew up in under five minutes with the loss of 862 men. 450 were rescued. *(Portsmouth Royal Naval Museum)*

HMS VALIANT was built by Fairfield and completed in 1916. She served with 5 BS which formed part of the Battle-Cruiser Fleet at Jutland and alternated between the Atlantic, Mediterranean and Home Fleets from 1919 to 1937 before being re-constructed between 1937 and 1939. In December 1939 she sailed to the West Indies to work-up and joined the Mediterranean Fleet in 1940. Each 15-inch gun weighed 97 tons and their shells weighed 1,920lb. *(Syd Goodman Collection)*

HMS VALIANT was reconstructed to the same standard as QUEEN ELIZABETH and was one of the first RN warships to be fitted with radar. She is seen here on 5 May 1943. She took part in the Battle of Matapan in 1941 and was hit twice by bombs off Crete. In December she was damaged by limpet mines attached by Italian frogmen in Alexandria and joined the Eastern Fleet in April 1942 after repairs. In 1943 she was refitted in the UK and joined Force H in the western Mediterranean to cover the Salerno landings, after which she rejoined the eastern Fleet in 1944 but returned to the UK for a refit that was not complete when the war ended. From 1945 she was used as part of HMS IMPERIEUSE, the Stoker Mechanics' training school at Devonport and was eventually scrapped in 1948. *(Syd Goodman Collection)*

HMS MALAYA was a gift to the Admiralty from the Federated Malay States. She was built by Armstrong at Elswick and joined 5 BS in time for Jutland, sustaining eight hits which killed 63 men and wounded 33; repairs were completed before the end of June. In June 1919 she visited Cherbourg for the Peace Celebrations and in 1920 carried the Allied Naval Commission on a tour of German naval ports to see that treaty obligations were being complied with. In 1921 she visited Malaya and joined the Atlantic Fleet on her return but was then sent to Istanbul as a show of strength following riots in Turkey. The Sultan took refuge on board and was conveyed to Malta for his own safety. She served in the Mediterranean, Atlantic and Home Fleets from 1924 to 1934 when she underwent a modernisation after which she returned to the Mediterranean Fleet. She is seen here entering Grand Harbour, Malta with Neutrality Patrol stripes on 'B' turret in July 1937. *(T. Ferrers-Walker Collection)*

HMS MALAYA in 1944; she had not been modernised to the same extent as her sisters but twin 4-inch Mark XIX mountings had been fitted to give a medium anti-aircraft capability. In 1939 she escorted the first Canadian troop convoy of the new war across the Atlantic. She moved to the Mediterranean in 1940 and bombarded Genoa in 1941. For some time she was flagship of Force H at Gibraltar and escorted the aircraft carriers ARK ROYAL and ARGUS on a number of 'runs' to ferry RAF aircraft to Malta. In 1944 she returned to UK waters and bombarded German targets ashore near St Malo after D-Day. She paid off into un-maintained reserve in 1945 and was scrapped in 1948. *(T. Ferrers-Walker Collection)*

HMS WARSPITE was one of the most famous warships ever to have served in the Royal Navy. She was built in Devonport Dockyard and completed in March 1915, joining 5 BS in time for Jutland. From 1919 to 1934 she alternated between the Atlantic and Mediterranean Fleets and then underwent a large-scale modernisation which lasted until 1937. In addition to improving the armament and armour, much weight and space was saved by replacing the original twenty-four boilers with six Admiralty three-drum types and new geared turbines. The work reputedly cost over £3 million, more than the original cost of the ship. Elevation of the 15-inch guns was increased from 20 degrees to 30 which improved the maximum range from 23,400 yards to 32,000. Unlike the later modernisations, she kept her original 6-inch guns. She rejoined the Mediterranean Fleet in 1937 and is seen here in that year with Neutrality Patrol markings on 'B' turret. *(Ken Kelly Collection)*

HMS WARSPITE provided heavy cover for Canadian troop convoys in 1939 and fought in the second Battle of Narvik in 1940. She became flagship of Admiral Cunningham, C-in-C Mediterranean Fleet, in 1940 and fought at Matapan. In operations off Crete she had over 400 bombs aimed at her and suffered damage which was repaired in the Bremerton Navy Yard in Seattle; she travelled there via Singapore and Pearl Harbour and returned via Sydney to join the Eastern Fleet at Colombo in 1942. In 1943 she returned to the Mediterranean and was hit by two radio-controlled bombs from a German aircraft which blew the bottom out of one of her boiler rooms. Repairs were incomplete when she was used a bombardment ship for the Normandy landings. She was mined and further damaged but continued in action, shooting at targets many miles inland. In November 1944 she supported landings by Royal Marines Commandos on Walcheren Island in the Scheldt Estuary, the last operation in a long and gallant career. She was approved to be scrapped in 1946 but on 4 April 1947 she broke lose from her tugs and ran aground in Prussia Cove in Cornwall. It proved impossible to move her so she was slowly broken up in situ.

(T. Ferrers-Walker Collection)

The 1913 construction programme included the 'R' class battleships. With only 40,000 hp they were slower than the Queen Elizabeths but their eight 15-inch 42 calibre guns were as effective - and they were good sea boats. HM Ships ROYAL SOVEREIGN and ROYAL OAK can be seen here turning in the Pentland Firth during manoeuvres in 1918 with other battleships in the background. Note the lack of smoke from the oil-burning 'R's compared with the coal-smoke from the others.

(Author's Collection)

HMS ROYAL SOVEREIGN off Philadelphia Navy Yard on 14 September 1943. She was built in Portsmouth Dockyard and completed in May 1916. Her belt armour and turret faces were up to 13-inch thick. She served in 1 BS of the Grand Fleet from 1916 to 1919 and with the Atlantic and Mediterranean Fleets from 1919 to 1936. After a period with the Home Fleet, she was Flagship of the Halifax Escort Force from 1939 to 1941 after which she joined the Eastern Fleet.

(Author's Collection)

HMS ROYAL SOVEREIGN returned to the UK from the Eastern Fleet in 1944 and is seen here in Scapa Flow on 29 June 1944 shortly before she was lent to the Soviet Navy and re-named ARCHANGELSK. She was not returned until 4 February 1949, after which she was sold for scrap.

(Author's Collection)

HMS ROYAL OAK was built in Devonport Dockyard and joined 1 BS of the Grand Fleet in May 1916 just in time to take part in the Battle of Jutland. She engaged enemy battle-cruisers and scored hits, a creditable performance for a ship that had little time to work-up to full efficiency. She served in the Atlantic, Mediterranean and Home Fleets between 1919 and 1939. She is seen here taking on board the body of Queen Maud for return to Norway on 24 November 1938. She was the wife of King Haakon of Norway, daughter of King Edward VII and sister of King George V and had died after an operation a few days earlier in a London hospital. Note the ensign at half-mast, the Norwegian flag at the yard and the black-draped brow.

(Ken Kelly Collection)

HMS ROYAL OAK leaving the Gladstone Dock in Liverpool. On 14 October 1939 she was torpedoed and sunk while at anchor in Scapa Flow by U-47 with the loss of 786 men. Her wreck lies in the north-east corner of the Flow off Scapa Bay and is a war memorial marked by a single buoy. She still (2009) leaks oil and RN divers survey her annually, attaching a new white ensign to the hull each time.

(Ken Kelly Collection)

HMS REVENGE photographed at high speed during combined Home and Mediterranean Fleet exercises off Gibraltar on 4 April 1938. She was built by Vickers and completed in March 1916. She served in 1 BS of the Grand Fleet and Admiral Burney transferred his flag to her when MARLBOROUGH was torpedoed. From November 1916 she was flagship of Admiral Madden, Second-in-Command of the Grand Fleet until 1919. From 1920 she served in the Atlantic, Mediterranean and Home Fleets until 1939 when she joined the convoy escort force based in Halifax. *(Ken Kelly Collection)*

HMS REVENGE in dry-dock in Portsmouth in 1939. She bombarded Cherbourg in September 1940 at 15,700 yards. In 1942 she was part of the Eastern Fleet and in 1943 she escorted an Australian troop convoy from Suez to Australia when forces were re-deployed from North Africa for operations against the Japanese in New Guinea. Later that year she returned to the UK and was reduced to reserve. In May 1944 she became part of HMS IMPERIEUSE, the stoker-mechanics' training establishment and she was sold for scrap in 1949.

(Ken Kelly Collection)

A close view of HMS RESOLUTION's forward 15-inch guns with ROYAL SOVEREIGN ahead during Mediterranean Fleet exercises in 1933. The 'R' class were the last to have 6-inch batteries in casemates on the main deck and among the first to include anti-aircraft guns, two single 3-inch, in their original armament. They had four 21-inch torpedo tubes with twenty reloads. She was built by Palmers at Jarrow and joined 1 BS of the Grand Fleet in August 1916, staying with it until 1919 when she joined 2 BS of the Atlantic Fleet. She alternated between the Atlantic, Mediterranean and Home Fleets until 1939.

(Ken Kelly Collection)

An immaculate HMS RESOLUTION in light grey Mediterranean paint during 1935. From 1939 she was used to escort Atlantic convoys against commerce raiders. In May 1940 she took part in operations off Norway and was bombed off Tjeldsundet. In August she joined Force M operating out of Freetown, Sierra Leone and was torpedoed off Dakar in September. After temporary repairs in Portsmouth she went to Philadelphia Navy Yard in March 1941 for full repairs and a refit which was completed in September. In February 1942 she became flagship of the Eastern Fleet and in February escorted an Australian troop convoy from Suez to Australia. She returned to the UK later in 1943 and paid off to form part of HMS IMPERIEUSE, the stoker-mechanics' training establishment, first in the Gareloch, then Southampton and finally Devonport. She was sold for scrap in 1948.

(T. Ferrers-Walker Collection)

HMS RAMILLIES off the Isle of Wight with hands fallen in for entering harbour. She was built by Beardmore but her rudder was damaged when she was launched and she had to be towed to Cammell Laird for repairs which delayed her completion until 1917. She served in 1 BS of the Grand Fleet until 1919 and then alternated between the Mediterranean, Atlantic and Home Fleets until 1939. She was never reconstructed but, as with all British battleships, a number of anti-aircraft weapons were added on an opportunity basis during the Second World War. Note the forecastle officer and those on the bridge saluting an unseen ship to port.

(Author's Collection)

HMS RAMILLIES in Plymouth Sound in 1943 following repairs after being hit by a torpedo off Diego Suarez. In 1939 she had covered the passage of the BEF to France and then joined Force J based at Aden to hunt for commerce raiders. She joined the Mediterranean Fleet in 1940, bombarded Bardia and was involved in the action off Cape Spartivento. In 1941 she escorted convoys between the UK and the Middle East and was ordered to the Western Atlantic in May during operations to contain BISMARCK. She joined the Eastern Fleet in 1942 until early 1944 with a brief period back in the UK for repairs. In early 1944 she returned to the UK to form part of the bombardment force for the landings in Normandy and the south of France, after which she paid off and was used as an accommodation ship attached to HMS VERNON in Portsmouth. She was sold for scrap in 1948.

(Author's Collection)

HMS REPULSE was originally laid down as a battleship of the 'R' class but was completed as a battle-cruiser. She was built by John Brown & Co on Clydebank in only nineteen months. Her machinery developed 126,000 hp giving her a speed of over 30 knots. Her main armament comprised six 15-inch guns with an unusual secondary battery of 4-inch guns in triple mountings. She joined 1 BCS in August 1916 and remained with it for the rest of the war. In 1922, she formed a Special Service Squadron with HMS HOOD to visit Rio de Janeiro for the Brazilian Centenary Celebrations and in 1923-24 the Squadron took the Prince of Wales on a world cruise that included visits to South Africa, Malaya, Australia, New Zealand, Canada, the USA and West Indies. From 1926 to 1932 she served in the Atlantic Fleet and then, after partial modernisation, the Mediterranean Fleet. In 1939 she escorted Atlantic convoys against surface raiders. *(Ken Kelly Collection)*

HMS REPULSE in her final paint scheme in December 1941. She saw action during the Norwegian Campaign in May 1940 and in October 1941 joined Force G in the East Indies Station, based on Colombo. In November she was ordered to join HMS PRINCE OF WALES to form Force Z based on Singapore and on 8 December 1941 left Singapore with PRINCE OF WALES and four destroyers to intercept a Japanese force reported off Kota Bharu. She was attacked by shore-based Japanese naval aircraft off Kuantan on 10 December 1941 and sank after suffering numerous bomb and torpedo hits despite a gallant defence without air cover. From a complement of 69 officers and 1,240 ratings, 42 officers (including Captain Tennant) and 754 ratings were rescued by destroyers. The RAF fighters from Singapore allocated for her defence arrived overhead as she sank.

(Syd Goodman Collection)

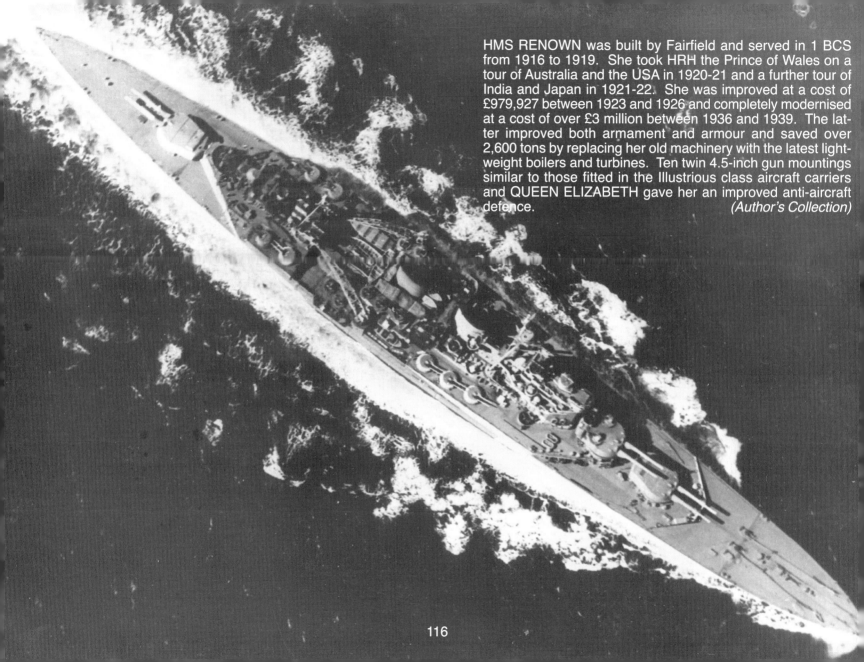

HMS RENOWN was built by Fairfield and served in 1 BCS from 1916 to 1919. She took HRH the Prince of Wales on a tour of Australia and the USA in 1920-21 and a further tour of India and Japan in 1921-22. She was improved at a cost of £979,927 between 1923 and 1926 and completely modernised at a cost of over £3 million between 1936 and 1939. The latter improved both armament and armour and saved over 2,600 tons by replacing her old machinery with the latest lightweight boilers and turbines. Ten twin 4.5-inch gun mountings similar to those fitted in the Illustrious class aircraft carriers and QUEEN ELIZABETH gave her an improved anti-aircraft defence. *(Author's Collection)*

HMS RENOWN in Trincomalee. She served as the Flagship of the Battle-Cruiser squadron, Home Fleet in 1939-40 and engaged SCHARNHORST and GNEISENAU off Norway in April 1940 but they were able to evade her in bad weather. In August she was flagship of Force H and supported carrier operations to fly RAF aircraft to Malta. In August 1943 she brought Winston Churchill and his party home from a meeting in Halifax and in November took him to Alexandria. From December 1943 she was in the Eastern Fleet but was ordered home 'with dispatch' on 30 March 1945 to form part of the Home Fleet when it accepted the surrender of the German Fleet, steaming 7,642miles at an average of 25 knots. She then had her complement reduced and joined the stoker-mechanic training establishment HMS IMPERIEUSE in Devonport. The last British battle-cruiser, she paid off in 1948 and was scrapped.

(Ken Kelly Collection)

HMS GLORIOUS was one of three 'large light cruisers' intended by Admiral Lord Fisher for his 'Baltic' Project. 786 feet long and capable of over 31 knots she was armed with four 15-inch guns in two turrets but only armoured to light cruiser standard. On completion in 1917 she was classified as a light battle-cruiser. She was built by Harland & Wolff in less than two years but was not regarded as a great asset by the Grand Fleet. She served as the flagship of 3 LCS and 1 CS in 1917/18 and saw action with enemy light forces in November 1917. After a period as a gunnery training ship in Devonport she was converted into an aircraft carrier from 1924.

(Syd Goodman Collection)

To date HMS HOOD is the longest warship, at 860 feet, to have served with the Royal Navy. She was built by John Brown & Co on Clydebank, cost £6,025,000 and was the last British capital ship to have a control top on the fore-mast. Commissioned in 1920 as the flagship of the BCS, she represented Britain at the Brazilian Centenary Celebrations in 1922 together with REPULSE and led the Special Service squadron which took HRH the Prince of Wales on a world tour in 1923-24 intended to show Britain's pre-eminent position as a naval power after the First World War. Between 1924 and 1926 she served in the Atlantic and Home Fleets and was considered to be such an important national asset that time could not be spared to modernise her.

(Portsmouth Royal Naval Museum)

HMS HOOD's ship's company painting her sides in Malta in the late 1930s, note the Neutrality Patrol stripes on 'B' turret. After the outbreak of war she served in the Home Fleet from 1939 to 1940 but in July became flagship of Force H and bombarded the French Fleet at Oran. In August she returned to the Home Fleet as flagship of the BCS under Vice Admiral L E Holland. She sailed with the new battleship PRINCE OF WALES to intercept BISMARCK and PRINZ EUGEN on 19 May 1941 and brought them to action on 24 May. After hits from enemy shells, she suffered a series of massive internal explosions and sank in minutes with only three survivors. Her wreck was located and filmed by a team led by David Mears in 2001.

(Ken Kelly Collection)

HMS RODNEY with her main armament trained to port. She was built by Cammell Laird and mounted nine 16-inch 45 calibre guns in three triple turrets disposed forward of the bridge and twelve new 6-inch guns in twin turrets. She had two 24.5-inch torpedo tubes and her belt armour was 14-inches thick with 16-inch turret faces. Each 16-inch gun weighed 103.5 tons and fired a shell weighing 2,461lb. A full broadside cost £700 at 1928 prices. She and her sister-ship NELSON were the first British battleships to mount 16-inch guns and triple turrets and the first to mount the secondary armament in turrets. She was completed in August 1927.

(Syd Goodman Collection)

HMS RODNEY in 1941 clearly showing the unusual arrangement of the main armament. She served with the Atlantic and Home Fleets between 1928 and 1941 and was flagship of the C-in-C from 1940. She hit BISMARCK with her third salvo in May 1941 and subsequently hit her repeatedly at decreasing range. She later served in the Mediterranean, covering the Allied landings in North Africa in 1942 and after returning to the UK she formed part of the bombardment force covering the Normandy landings, during which she bombarded German forces in Caen, some miles inland. In August spotting aircraft helped her guns destroy a German battery in Alderney which could not be seen from the ship. She had no significant refit after 1942 but steamed 156,000 miles between then and the end of the war. Worn out and having suffered an increasing number of break-downs, she saw no further service and was sold for scrap in 1948. *(Syd Goodman Collection)*

HMS NELSON on 8 January 1945 after her long refit in Philadelphia Navy Yard. She was built by Vickers-Armstrong on the Tyne and was commissioned in June 1927. She became flagship of the Atlantic Fleet and for the next fourteen years flew the flags of seven successive Commanders-in-Chief of the Atlantic and Home Fleets. Mined in 1939 she played an important part in the Second World War after repairs. She escorted convoys to Malta including 'Pedestal', covered the North African landings and the invasions of Sicily and Italy. The Italian surrender, signed by General Eisenhower and Marshal Badoglio, took place on board in Malta on 29 September 1943. She was with the British bombardment force during the Normandy landings and was repaired in Philadelphia Navy Yard after further mine damage. In 1945 she moved to the East Indies Fleet and the surrender of Japanese forces in Malaya was signed in Penang on the same table as that used for the surrender of Italy. She returned to the UK to become flagship of the Home Fleet again in 1945, transferred to the Home Fleet Training Squadron in 1946 and paid off in 1948. Used as a bombing target before being scrapped in 1949. *(Author's Collection)*

HMS KING GEORGE V sailing from Guam in 1945. The Admiralty had intended to name her King George VI following the tradition that the first capital ship laid down in a new reign is named after the sovereign. King George VI insisted, however, that she should be named KG V in honour of his father, despite the fact that there had already been a battleship with that name; his wish was respected. Her main armament was radical and comprised ten 14-inch guns in two quadruple and one twin turret and sixteen 5.25-inch guns in eight turrets. A large number of close-range weapons were added for use against aircraft. She was the first British battleship to mount 14-inch guns since HMS CANADA in 1915, to have dual purpose high and low-angle secondary armament and to be designed with a catapult and hangars to operate aircraft - up to four Walrus amphibians.

(Author's Collection)

HMS KING GEORGE V with the Training Squadron in 1948. She completed in 1940 and relieved NELSON as flagship of the Home Fleet in April 1941; was in action against BISMARCK in May 1941 and covered a number of convoys to North Russia in 1942-43. In 1942 she accidentally rammed and sank the destroyer PUNJABI and was damaged both by the impact and the detonation of depth charges. After leaving the Home Fleet she covered landings in Sicily in 1943 and occupied Taranto in September. In 1944 she was refitted to prepare her for service in the Far East. *(Syd Goodman Collection)*

In 1945 HMS KING GEORGE V became the flagship of the Vice-Admiral Second-in-Command, British Pacific Fleet and was present when carrier-borne aircraft struck at targets in Sumatra, the Sakashima Islands and mainland Japan. She bombarded the Hitachi area of Honshu in July and was present at the Japanese surrender in Tokyo Bay on 2 September. In March 1946 she returned to the UK and relieved NELSON as flagship of the Home Fleet for the second time. From 1947 to 1950 she served in the Home Fleet BS, but not as Flagship, and was then laid up in the Gareloch; one of the first capital ships to be 'cocooned' in a state of preservation. In 1958 she was towed to Dalmuir to be broken up for scrap; the hull was eventually scrapped at Troon.

(Author's Collection)

HMS PRINCE OF WALES, seen here at anchor in August 1941, was built by Cammell Laird and completed in March 1941. She took part in the BISMARCK action despite not being fully worked up and with civilian staff still working on the gun mountings. She scored two hits, one of which caused BISMARCK to leak oil and attempt to return to harbour. In July 1941 she conveyed Winston Churchill and his party to Placentia Bay in Newfoundland for the Atlantic Charter Conference with President Roosevelt.

(Syd Goodman Collection)

HMS PRINCE OF WALES in September 1941 weighing anchor; note the cable party hosing down the cable in the port hawse-pipe. In November she was ordered to join REPULSE in Singapore to act as what the Prime Minister believed would be a deterrent against Japanese war plans in the Far East. (*T. Ferrers-Walker Collection*)

HMS PRINCE OF WALES coming alongside in Singapore Naval base in December 1941. The flag in the fore-ground marks the bow position of the allocated berth. On 10 December she was sunk off Kuantan together with REPULSE when they were attacked by shore-based Japanese naval aircraft. An early torpedo hit on the port 'A' bracket made her difficult to control and she received a number of further torpedo and bomb hits. 1,285 sailors were rescued by destroyers out of a total ship's company and staff of 1,612. Neither Admiral Phillips nor Captain Leach survived. *(Author's Collection)*

HMS HOWE during sea trials in May 1942. She was built by Fairfield and commissioned in August 1942. Her aircraft cranes are seen here raised clear above the athwartship catapult between the funnels. She joined the Home Fleet in 1942, the Mediterranean Fleet in 1943 and the Eastern Fleet in 1944.

(Author's Collection)

HMS HOWE became the flagship of the British Pacific Fleet on its formation in November 1944 and was in Sydney in January 1945. She took part in several bombardments before leaving for refit in South Africa in June and returned to the UK in January 1946, after which she joined the Home Fleet Training Squadron. *(T. Ferrers-Walker Collection)*

HMS HOWE entering the basin in Devonport Dockyard on 19 May 1948 after Home Fleet exercises off the Norwegian coast. The battleship in the background is KING GEORGE V and the maintenance carrier UNICORN and a light fleet carrier are visible at buoys in the River Tamar. In 1950 Howe became the HQ ship for the Senior Officer, Reserve Fleet in Portsmouth and in 1952 she returned to Devonport for the remainder of her service life. She was the only ship of her class not to be laid up in the Gareloch and was broken up at Inverkeithing in 1958.

(Syd Goodman Collection)

HMS DUKE OF YORK was originally to have been named ANSON but the Admiralty re-named her as a mark of respect to King George VI, who had been Duke of York before he unexpectedly became King, after he insisted on the lead ship of the class being named after his father. She was built by John Brown on Clydebank and joined the Home Fleet on completion in November 1941. She covered a number of Russian convoys and, as flagship of the Admiral Fraser, the C-in-C Home Fleet, sank the SCHARNHORST in the Battle of North Cape in December 1943; the last big-gun action fought by the Royal Navy. She sailed for the British Pacific Fleet after the defeat of Germany and was Admiral Fraser's flagship again at the Japanese surrender in Tokyo Bay on 2 September 1945. *(Author's Collection)*

HMS DUKE OF YORK in Portland Harbour in September 1948. She had returned to the UK in July 1946 and served as the flagship of the Home Fleet from 1947. In 1949 she became flagship of the Reserve Fleet until 1951 when she was 'cocooned' and laid up in the Gareloch. She was broken up at Faslane in 1958. *(Author's Collection)*

This impressive photograph of HMS ANSON was taken during speed trials in October 1942. She was built by Swan Hunter and joined the Home Fleet on completion, providing cover for a number of convoys to North Russia. She joined the British Pacific Fleet in 1945, too late to see action against the Japanese mainland but she was present at the surrender of Japanese forces in Hong Kong on 16 September 1945 and served for a time as British guardship in Tokyo Bay. She returned to Australia in January 1946 and the UK in July that year.

(Author's Collection)

HMS ANSON in October 1948. She was refitted after her return from the Pacific and became the flagship of the Home Fleet Training Squadron for a time. Note that the catapult has been removed and replaced by structure for extra accommodation on top of which the ship's boats are stowed. The large cranes were retained to lift the boats outboard. *(Author's Collection)*

HMS ANSON in 1945. The 14-inch guns could fire two rounds per minute out to 36,000 yards. The quadruple turrets weighed 1,550 and the twin 900 tons. ANSON was the only ship of her class to be fitted with Mark VI directors for her 5.25-inch guns. Her post-war career was brief; 'cocooned' in the Gareloch in 1950 and sold for scrap in 1957.

(Syd Goodman Collection)

HMS VANGUARD was the last British battleship to be built. She was a 'one-off', designed to make use of the 15-inch guns and mountings removed from COURAGEOUS and GLORIOUS when they were converted into aircraft carriers, modified to allow greater elevation and thus longer range. She is seen here being taken into dry-dock in Devonport for post-completion defect rectification. The ship visible in the next dock is HMS TERRIBLE, the only aircraft carrier ever to be built in a Royal Dockyard, which was subsequently sold to Australia as HMAS SYDNEY.

(*Syd Goodman Collection*)

HMS VANGUARD was an outstanding sea-boat because of the long, flared forecastle and performed better than the USN Iowa class battleships in early NATO exercises in the Atlantic winter. Seen here in 1946, she was the heaviest and most expensive British warship ever built at the time of her completion. Her armament comprised eight 15-inch and sixteen 5.25-inch guns. Fifty-nine 40mm Bofors close-range anti-aircraft guns were fitted in sextuple, twin and single mountings. Her armoured belt was up to 14-inch thick and the turret faces were 13-inch.

(Syd Goodman Collection)

HMS VANGUARD returning to Devonport Dockyard after a shake-down cruise to the Mediterranean. She has been fitted for the Royal Tour of South Africa by King George VI, Queen Elizabeth and the two Princesses; note the glazed accommodation added for the Royal Party on the deck forward of 'X' turret. *(Syd Goodman Collection)*

HMS VANGUARD firing a salute to Queen Elizabeth II embarked in the Royal Yacht BRITANNIA, on 14 May 1954. From 1950 to 1954 VANGUARD was the flagship of the Home Fleet. In 1955 she became the flagship of the Reserve Fleet and NATO Headquarters in Portsmouth. She was de-commissioned in June 1960 and towed out of Portsmouth on 4 August but ran aground by the 'Still and West-Country' public house. It took eight tugs to pull her clear and complete the journey to Faslane. It seems that, like WARSPITE and others, she didn't want to go but she was broken up soon afterwards, ending an era of metal battleships that had lasted almost exactly 100 years. *(Author's Collection)*

TABLE OF BATTLESHIP PARTICULARS

Showing Ships in class, full load displacement, length overall, horse-power, speed, main armament and cost. The figures are for a representative ship of the class as built, other units may vary slightly and the majority of ships were significantly altered during their service lives.

Warrior, Black Prince

9,210 tons	380ft	5,270hp	14 knots	26 x 28pdr	10 x 110pdr BL	4 x 70pdr BL	£377,292

Defence, Resistance

6,150 tons	280ft	2,540hp	10 knots	8 x 7-inch BL	10 x 68pdr	4 x 5-inch BL	£258,120

Hector, Valiant

7,000 tons	280ft	3,260hp	12 knots	4 x 7-inch BL	20 x 68pdr		£294,000

Achilles

6,670 tons	380ft	5,720hp	14 knots	20 x 100pdr			£469,572

Royal Oak

6,360 tons	273ft	800hp	12 knots	11 x 7-inch BLR	24 x 68pdr		£254,537

Prince Consort, Caledonia, Ocean

3,715 tons	252ft	1,000hp	12 knots	7 x 7-inch BLR	8 x 100pdr	16 x 68pdr	£266,173

Minotaur, Agincourt, Northumberland

10,690 tons	400ft	6,700hp	14 knots	4 x 9-inch MLR	24 x 7-inch MLR	8 x 24pdr	£478,855

Prince Albert							
3,880 tons	240ft	2,130hp	11 knots	4 x 9-inch MLR			£208,345
Royal Sovereign							
5,080 tons	240ft	2,460hp	11 knots	5 x 10.5-inch ML			£180,572
Scorpion, Wivern							
2,750 tons	224ft	1,450hp	10 knots	4 x 9-inch MLR			£111,614
Research, Enterprise, Favourite, Lord Warden, Lord Clyde							
1,200 tons	185ft	1,040hp	10 knots	4 x 100pdr			£71,287
Pallas, Bellerophon							
3,794 tons	225ft	3,580hp	13 knots	2 x 7-inch BL	4 x 7-inch MLR		£190,403
Zealous, Royal Alfred, Penelope							
6,100 tons	252ft	3,450hp	11 knots	20 x 7-inch MLR			£239,258
Hercules							
8,680 tons	325ft	6,750hp	14 knots	8 x 10-inch MLR	2 x 9-inch MLR	4 x 7-inch MLR	£377,008
Monarch							
8,300 tons	330ft	7,840hp	15 knots	4 x 12-inch MLR	3 x 7-inch MLR		£354,575
Captain							
7,767 tons	320ft	5,400hp	14 knots	4 x 12-inch MLR	2 x 7-inch MLR		£335,518

Repulse							
6,190 tons	252ft	3,350hp	12 knots	12 x 8-inch MLR			£183,640

Audacious, Invincible, Iron Duke, Vanguard							
6,010 tons	280ft	4,830hp	13 knots	10 x 9-inch MLR	4 x 6-inch MLR		£256,291

Swiftsure, Triumph							
6,910 tons	280ft	4,830hp	13 knots	10 x 9-inch MLR	4 x 6-inch MLR		£257,081

Sultan							
9,290 tons	325ft	7,720hp	14 knots	8 x 10-inch MLR	4 x 9-inch MLR		£374,777

Cerberus, Magdala							
3,340 tons	225ft	1,370hp	10 knots	4 x 10-inch MLR			£117,556

Abyssinia							
2,900 tons	225ft	1,200hp	9 knots	4 x 10-inch MLR			Unknown

Glatton							
4,910 tons	245ft	2,870hp	12 knots	2 x 12-inch MLR			£223,101

Hotspur							
4,010 tons	235ft	3,500hp	12 knots	1 x 12-inch MLR	2 x 64pdr MLR		£175,995

Rupert							
5,440 tons	250ft	4,200hp	13 knots	2 x 10-inch MLR	2 x 64pdr MLR		£239,197

Devastation, Thunderer

9,330 tons	285ft	6,650hp	13 knots	4 x 10-inch BL			£361,438

Dreadnought

10,886 tons	320ft	8,210hp	14 knots	4 x 12.5-inch MLR			£619,739

Cyclops, Gorgon, Hecate, Hydra

3,480 tons	225ft	1,660hp	11 knots	4 x 10-inch MLR			£156,782

Alexandra

9,490 tons	325ft	8,610hp	15 knots	2 x 11-inch MLR	10 x 10-inch MLR	6 x 13cwt BL	£538,293

Temeraire

8,540 tons	285ft	7,520hp	14 knots	4 x 11-inch MLR	4 x 10-inch MLR	6 x 20pdr	£489,822

Shannon

5,390 tons	260ft	3,370hp	12 knots	2 x 10-inch MLR	7 x 9-inch MLR		£302,707

Nelson, Northampton

7,630 tons	280ft	6,624hp	14 knots	4 x 10-inch MLR	8 x 9-inch MLR		£411,302

Inflexible

11,880 tons	320ft	8,407hp	14 knots	4 x 16-inch MLR			£812,485

Ajax, Agamemnon

8,510 tons	280ft	6,000hp	13 knots	4 x 12.5-inch MLR	2 x 6-inch BL		£548,393

Belleisle, Orion

4,870 tons	245ft	3,200hp	12 knots	4 x 12-inch MLR	4 x 20pdr MLR		£267,179

Superb

9,710 tons	332ft	6,580hp	13 knots	16 x 10-inch MLR	6 x 20pdr BL		£531,846

Neptune

9,310 tons	300ft	7,993hp	14 knots	4 x 12-inch MLR	2 x 9-inch MLR		£689,172

Colossus, Edinburgh

9,150 tons	325ft	7,488hp	16 knots	4 x 12-inch BL	5 x 6-inch BL		£661,716

Conqueror, Hero

6,200 tons	270ft	4,500hp	14 knots	2 x 12-inch BL	4 x 6-inch BL		£401,991

Collingwood

9,500 tons	325ft	7,000hp	15 knots	4 x 12-inch BL	6 x 6-inch BL		£636,996

Imperieuse, Warspite

8,500 tons	315ft	8,000hp	16 knots	4 x 9.2-inch BL	10 x 6-inch BL		£543,758

Anson, Camperdown, Howe, Rodney

10,600 tons	330ft	7,500hp	15 knots	4 x 13.5-inch	6 x 6-inch		£662,582

Benbow

10,600 tons	330ft	11,500hp	17 knots	2 x 16.25-inch	10 x 6-inch		£764,022

Sans Pareil, Victoria							
11,020 tons	340ft	14,000hp	17 knots	2 x 16.25-inch	1 x 10-inch	12 x 6-inch	£844,922

Nile, Trafalgar							
12,590 tons	345ft	12,000hp	16 knots	4 x 13.5-inch	6 x 4.7-inch		£885,718

Empress of India, Ramillies, Repulse, Resolution, Revenge, Royal Oak, Royal Sovereign							
15,585 tons	380ft	13,360hp	18 knots	4 x 13.5-inch	10 x 6-inch		£913,986

Hood							
15,588 tons	380ft	11,000hp	16 knots	4 x 13.5-inch	10 x 6-inch		£926,396

Barfleur, Centurion							
10,500 tons	360ft	13,000hp	18 knots	4 x 10-inch	10 x 4.7-inch		£533,666

Renown							
12,350 tons	380ft	12,000hp	18 knots	4 x 10-inch	10 x 6-inch		£751,706

Majestic, Magnificent, Hannibal, Prince George, Victorious, Jupiter, Mars, Caesar, Illustrious							
16,060 tons	390ft	12,000hp	17 knots	4 x 12-inch	12 x 6-inch		£986,482

Canopus, Glory, Albion, Goliath, Ocean, Vengeance							
14,320 tons	390ft	13,500hp	18 knots	4 x 12-inch	12 x 6-inch		£866,516

Formidable, Irresistible, Implacable							
15,000 tons	400ft	15,000hp	18 knots	4 x 12-inch	12 x 6-inch		£1,096,745

Bulwark, London, Venerable, Queen, Prince of Wales							
15,640 tons	400ft	15,000hp	18 knots	4 x 12-inch	12 x 6-inch		£1,036,393

Duncan, Cornwallis, Exmouth, Russell, Albemarle, Montagu							
15,100 tons	405ft	18,000hp	19 knots	4 x 12-inch	12 x 6-inch		£1,093,000

King Edward VII, Dominion, Commonwealth, Hindustan, New Zealand (later Zealandia), Africa, Britannia, Hibernia							
15,639 tons	454ft	18,000hp	18 knots	4 x 12-inch	4 x 9.2-inch	10 x 6-inch	£1,382,675

Swiftsure, Triumph							
13,840 tons	480ft	12,500hp	19 knots	4 x 10-inch	14 x 7.5-inch		£846,596

Lord Nelson, Agamemnon							
16,090 tons	444ft	16,750hp	18 knots	4 x 12-inch	10 x 9.2-inch		£1,651,139

Dreadnought							
21,845 tons	527ft	23,000hp	21 knots	10 x 12-inch			£1,783,883

Invincible, Inflexible, Indomitable							
20,135 tons	567ft	41,000hp	25 knots	8 x 12-inch	16 x 4-inch	1 x 3-inch	£1,725,739

Bellerophon, Superb, Temeraire							
22,102 tons	526ft	23,000hp	21 knots	10 x 12-inch	16 x 4-inch		£1,765,342

St Vincent, Collingwood, Vanguard							
23,030 tons	536ft	24,500hp	21 knots	10 x 12-inch	20 x 4-inch		£1,754,615

Neptune

22,720 tons	546ft	25,000hp	21 knots	10 x 12-inch	16 x 4-inch		£1,668,916

Indefatigable, Australia, New Zealand

22,080 tons	590ft	44,000hp	25 knots	8 x 12-inch	16 x 4-inch		£1,641,500

Colossus, Hercules

23,050 tons	546ft	25,000hp	21 knots	10 x 12-inch	16 x 4-inch		£1,672,102

Conqueror, Monarch, Orion, Thunderer

25,870 tons	581ft	27,000hp	21 knots	10 x 13.5-inch	16 x 4-inch		£1,918,773

Lion, Princess Royal, Queen Mary

29,680 tons	700ft	70,000hp	27 knots	8 x 13.5-inch	16 x 4-inch		£2,086,458

King George V, Centurion, Audacious, Ajax

25,700 tons	597ft	31,000hp	22 knots	10 x 13.5-inch	16 x 4-inch		£1,960,000

Iron Duke, Marlborough, Benbow, Emperor of India

30,380 tons	623ft	29,000hp	21 knots	10 x 13.5-inch	12 x 6-inch		£1,891,122

Tiger

35,160 tons	704ft	85,000hp	28 knots	8 x 13.5-inch	12 x 6-inch		£2,593,100

Queen Elizabeth, Barham, Malaya, Valiant, Warspite

33,000 tons	646ft	75,000hp	24 knots	8 x 15-inch	14 x 6-inch		£2,500,000

Royal Sovereign, Royal Oak, Revenge, Resolution, Ramillies

| 31,200 tons | 624ft | 40,000hp | 21 knots | 8 x 15-inch | 14 x 6-inch | | £2,500,000 |

Erin

| 25,250 tons | 559ft | 26,500hp | 21 knots | 10 x 13.5-inch | 16 x 6-inch | | £2,500,000 |

Agincourt

| 30,250 tons | 671ft | 34,000hp | 22 knots | 14 x 12-inch | 20 x 6-inch | | £2,900,000 |

Canada

| 32,120 tons | 661ft | 37,000hp | 23 knots | 10 x 14-inch | 16 x 6-inch | | £2,500,000 |

Renown, Repulse

| 32,727 tons | 794ft | 126,000hp | 32 knots | 6 x 15-inch | 17 x 4-inch | 2 x 3-inch | £3,117,204 |

Hood

| 45,200 tons | 860ft | 144,000hp | 31 knots | 8 x 15-inch | 12 x 5.5-inch | 4 x 4-inch | £6,025,000 |

Nelson, Rodney

| 38,000 tons | 710ft | 45,000hp | 23 knots | 9 x 16-inch | 12 x 6-inch | 6 x 4.7-inch | £7,504,055 |

King George V, Prince of Wales, Duke of York, Anson, Howe

| 44,460 tons | 745ft | 125,000hp | 29 knots | 10 x 14-inch | 16 x 5.25-inch | | £7,493,000 |

Vanguard

| 51,420 tons | 814ft | 130,000hp | 30 knots | 8 x 15-inch | 16 x 5.25-inch | 59 x 40mm | £11,000,000 |

INDEX

RODNEY (1927)	121,122	SUPERB (1909)	62	VANGUARD (1946)	138,139,140,141
ROYAL OAK (1894)	32	SWIFTSURE (1904)	54	VENGEANCE (1902)	43
ROYAL OAK (1916)	103,106,107			VICTORIA (1890)	29
ROYAL SOVEREIGN (1892)	33	TEMERAIRE (1909)	63		
ROYAL SOVEREIGN (1916)	103,104,105	THUNDERER (1912)	75	WARRIOR (1861)	4
		TIGER (1914)	88	WARSPITE (1888)	26
ST VINCENT (1909)	64	TRAFALGAR (1890)	30	WARSPITE (1915)	101,102
SANS PAREIL (1891)	28	TRIUMPH (1904)	53		
SCORPION (1865)	6			ZEALANDIA (1905)	52
SULTAN (1871)	12	VALIANT (1916)	97,98		
SUPERB (1880)	20	VANGUARD (1910)	65		

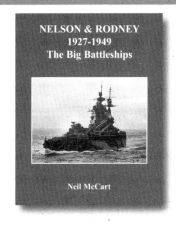